This is the
MINIATURE
SCHNAUZER

Louise Ziegler Spirer - Herbert F. Spirer

ISBN 0-87666-339-0

Distributed in the UNITED STATES by T.F.H. Publications, Inc., 211 West
Sylvania Avenue, Neptune City, NJ 07753; in CANADA by H & L Pet Supplies
Inc., 27 Kingston Crescent, Kitchener, Ontario N2B 2T6; Rolf C. Hagen Ltd.,
3225 Sartelon Street, Montreal 382 Quebec; in ENGLAND by T.F.H. (Great
Britain) Ltd., 11 Ormside Way, Holmethorpe Industrial Estate, Redhill, Sur-
rey RH1 2PX; in AUSTRALIA AND THE SOUTH PACIFIC by T.F.H. (Australia)
Pty. Ltd., Box 149, Brookvale 2100 N.S.W., Australia; in NEW ZEALAND by
Ross Haines & Son, Ltd., 18 Monmouth Street, Grey Lynn, Auckland 2 New
Zealand; in SINGAPORE AND MALAYSIA by MPH Distributors Pte., 71-77
Stamford Road, Singapore 0617; in the PHILIPPINES by Bio-Research, 5
Lippay Street, San Lorenzo Village, Makati, Rizal; in SOUTH AFRICA by
Multipet Pty. Ltd., 30 Turners Avenue, Durban 4001. Published by T.F.H.
Publications Inc., Ltd., the British Crown Colony of Hong Kong.

CONTENTS

THE MINIATURE SCHNAUZER

General instructive photographs by Louise Brown Van der Meid through the cooperation of Isabel Swartz, Lila Jones, Applegarth's Ge'Nel Kennels, Mildred Knecht, William Chandler, Ronald Harrabill, and Margie Bush.

Drawings by Ernest H. Hart.

Acknowledgements

Special thanks are due to Girleen Kenny and Matthew Kenny for invaluable assistance in the editing, typing, and checking that went into the preparation of this book.

The advice of Jack Patterson, D.V.M., has been gratefully received and we have endeavored to live up to his high standards.

The latest official Miniature Schnauzer standards were supplied to us by the American Miniature Schnauzer Club.

Chapter I
History

INTRODUCTION

Today is the day you bring home the dog of your dreams! The whole family is turned out, flags in hand, red carpet laid to the front door, bunting flying in the breeze. We envy you the excitement of this all-important day when you bring home your purebred Miniature Schnauzer.

But along with the flags and bunting, we hope that you have prepared for your new pet in other ways. Is there a bed ready for him (or her)? Do you have some warm milk or formula prepared? Have you set aside some of this day to welcome your tiny dog and show him around his new home? He may be lonely—for his mother, his brothers and sisters, the familiar bed in the kennel. A little cuddling and warmth and you and your new puppy will soon be sure of each other and the best of friends.

The joys and the responsibilities of dogdom are now yours. You are responsible for this new member of the household. You will care for him, feed, train, groom, and house him. In time of illness you must call the veterinarian and help him in the care of your pet. You are responsible now, both to yourself and your community, for a well-trained, healthy, and happy dog.

In return, your dog will respond with love. He will guard your household and your family and will give all of you great enjoyment and pleasure.

Miniature Schnauzer breeders have spent much time and energy with their dogs; they have bred them scientifically, fed the mother properly and seen that her litter has had a good start in life with the right food and medical care. But no amount of early care on the part of the breeder can make up for what you—the dog owner—must do to raise a healthy dog.

This book was written to help you in the day-to-day care of your dog. We hope that you will read it through and use the index for a handy reference in case of special problems. This is a practical book and should be supplemented by personal contact with a licensed veterinarian.

The most important thing is to enjoy your dog. He is one of the most lovable dogs in the world. His alert eyes, handsome grooming, attractive coloring, and dashing nature make him an ideal dog for all families. Well-cared for and gently treated, he will always be a pleasure.

The dog has been man's best friend for many thousands of years. He has not only been his friend but also his companion, guardian, shepherd, and messenger boy as well. The dog's intelligence and

English Ch. Gosmore Hat Trick, owned by Mrs. A. B. Dallison. Photo by C. M. Cooke & Son.

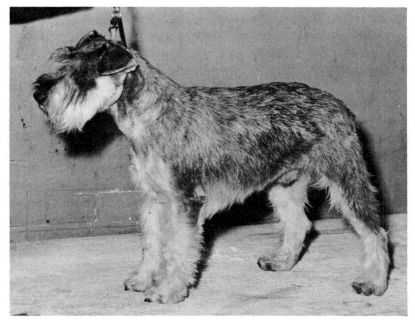

English Ch. Rannook Dune Randolph of Appeline, owned by D. H. Appleton. Photo by C. M. Cooke & Son.

loyalty have served man well; in return, man has taken care of his pet —housed and fed him, written and sung songs about him and painted his picture.

ANCIENT HISTORY

The ancient dog was closely related to the wolf. They had common ancestors and common features. The wild ancient dogs hunted in packs, as wolves still do, and coöperated to find food, using their cunning and physical strength to run down game. By the time man and dog joined forces, there were several fairly distinct types such as Hound, Terrier (the Schnauzer is a member of this ancient type) and Shepherd. We do not know the exact date when the dog was domesticated, but wall paintings in the prehistoric cave dwellings of Southern France show a Shepherd or Alsatian type of dog accompanying man and hunting wild animals. These drawings are believed to be more than 50,000 years old. Dog remains were found in neolithic England, and primitive men in Switzerland and Ireland used hunters.

English Ch. Deltone Deloklahoma, owned by S. J. Burke. Photo by C. M. Cooke & Son.

In the colder climates, dogs resembling Samoyeds and Elkhounds were living in Scandinavia 6,000 years ago, companions and hunters for the earliest Vikings. On the other side of the world, archaeologists have uncovered dog remains in the tomb of an Incan high priestess.

In more recent times, Egyptian tombs 3,000 years old have yielded many paintings depicting life in ancient Egypt. These showed that the Egyptians used dogs extensively for herding sheep, hunting and companionship. It is now believed that the Terrier class, as we know it, was developed in the Egypt of the Pharaohs.

The Greeks left the western world a glorious heritage in art, literature, and architecture, including many scenes and stories about dogs. Homer celebrates the dog Argus in the *Odyssey* and tells of dogs which can perceive the supernatural. The Greeks put one of these dogs, Sirius, in the heavens as the Dog Star, and many dogs appear in statues. Alexander the Great named a city after his favorite dog,

An unclipped and unstripped Miniature Schnauzer.

Peritas, surely a signal honor. Archaeologists have uncovered numerous memorial plaques from Greece and Rome which are tributes to dogs from their fond masters.

The Persians used dogs for hunting, and some of their most ancient tales tell of dogs hunting down not only small game but also lions, giraffes, and even elephants.

By Roman times, there were six fairly distinct types of dogs: Sheep-herders, such as Huskies and Chows; Scent Hounds (the Romans used Bloodhounds for hunting); Greyhounds, like the Saluki and Afghan; sporting or Spaniel types, like the Setter, Retriever and Poodle; and war dogs, such as the Bulldog, Great Dane and Boxer. They may also have had Terrier types for stable and barn, as well as housedogs or pet toy dogs, as the seventh type which is not clearly defined. Naturally, these different types of dogs were not purebred in today's sense, but they closely resembled their modern descendants.

Most American Miniature Schnauzers have cropped ears.

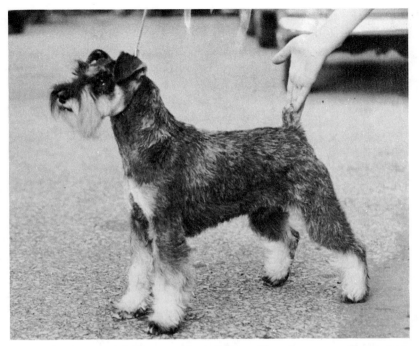

English Ch. Gosmore L.B.W., owned by A. Dallison. Note the uncropped ears of this champion. Photo by C. M. Cooke & Son.

HISTORY OF THE MINIATURE SCHNAUZER

The history of the Miniature Schnauzer is, first of all, the history of the Schnauzer itself, a member of the class of Terriers. The Moorland dog, who lived in the Bronze Age, was most likely the ancient ancestor of the Terrier, as well as of the Poodle and Spitz. As we saw, Terriers were found in Egypt and other Near Eastern countries and migrated to Europe. "Terrier" is taken from the Latin word *terrarus*, meaning "earth."

By the 15th century, a dog strongly resembling the Schnauzer could be found in many European homes and on farms. Such a dog is often seen in paintings by the early Renaissance artists. A 15th century artist, Lucas Cranach the Elder, pictured a dog much like today's

Schnauzer in his famous painting *The Crown of Thorns*, in which the dog appears to be about 16 inches high.

Perhaps the most famous artist to show our dog was Albrecht Dürer (1471-1528). In a series of pictures, dating over 10 or 12 years, he shows the same dog in various poses. Art historians believe that it was Dürer's studio dog which appears in *The Madonna With Many Animals* (1492); *Lovers* (1496) in which the dog appears with a couple; *The Martyrdom of John*, where the dog seems to be guarding the painter's initials in one corner, and *The Bearing of the Cross*. The last painting in which the dog appears is *Christ Before Caiphas* (1504). By this time the dog must have been 10 or 12 years old, a ripe old age for a dog in those days. It is likely that Dürer kept the dog as a companion and a vermin catcher. An old 14th century manuscript shows both men and terrier-like dogs digging for a fox.

Later on, dogs like the Schnauzer appear in Rembrandt's paintings. Undoubtedly, these likeable Terriers, so useful as ratters in crowded cities with inadequate sanitation, were favorite household pets.

But it wasn't until the late 1880's that breeders began to systematically breed the Schnauzer, and later the Miniature Schnauzer. The early purebred Schnauzers appear to be a mixture of black Poodle and wolf-gray Spitz. Mixed in is some Old German Pinscher stock, bringing in black-and-tan and fawn coloration, and perhaps a pinch of the Wurttenberg droving dogs. Wurttenberg is considered by many to be the cradle of German dogs, as so many were bred in this district. These early Schnauzers were pepper-and-salt, black-and-tan and occasionally solid black.

The German Pinscher Club, founded in 1895, included both the wire-haired and smooth-haired dogs. Many different types are included under the Pinscher label, such as the smooth-haired English Terrier, Fox Terrier, Black-and-Tan Terrier and long-haired Terriers. It was later that this club split into Schnauzer and Pinscher clubs, and still later that the Schnauzer and Miniature Schnauzer fanciers formed separate clubs.

Two of the early Schnauzer breeders were Max Hartenstein and Georg Goeller. Herr Goeller, whose luxuriant whiskers and eyebrows made him resemble his dogs, refused to divulge how he obtained the pepper-and-salt coats he bred into his dogs, thereby enraging some of the local breeders who wished to learn the secret. The dogs were accepted by 1890 and the first standards established in Germany. These standards, written for the German Short-haired

English Ch. Gosmore Wicket Keeper, owned by L. Rees. Photo by C. M. Cooke & Son.

English Ch. Chorltonville Quintin Bonus, owned by S. E. Whiteley. Photo by C. M. Cooke & Son.

English Ch. Deltone Delsanta Luella, owned by Mrs. D. Crowe. Photo by C. M. Cooke & Son.

English Ch. Eastwight Sea Nymph, owned by Miss P. Morrison-Bell. Photo by C. M. Cooke & Son.

Pinscher, included both the smooth-haired and the wire-haired types. The standard ruled that long wavy hair and curly matted hair were disallowed. Later the Pinschers and Schnauzers diverged into separate classes. In German, *Schnauzer* means snout or muzzle.

The Miniature Schnauzer, with all these distinguished ancestors, was the result of a deliberate cross between the Affenpinscher, or Monkey-faced Pinscher, and a rather smallish standard Schnauzer. Just why some breeder wished to breed smaller Schnauzers is not known, but he may have had in mind today's small (but not tiny), rugged individual, the Miniature Schnauzer. It is possible that city dwellers, crowded into houses or apartments, wanted a small pet (or perhaps a small rat catcher), and encouraged the propagation of miniature dogs. The early Affenpinscher was black, with upstanding ears, a wire-haired coat and a monkey-like face. Some of the early Miniature Schnauzer champions, such as Jocco-Firlda (PB 604) show the influence of this breed. It was not until breeders eliminated

English Ch. Eastwight Seasprite, owned by Miss P. Morrison-Bell. Photo by C. M. Cooke & Son.

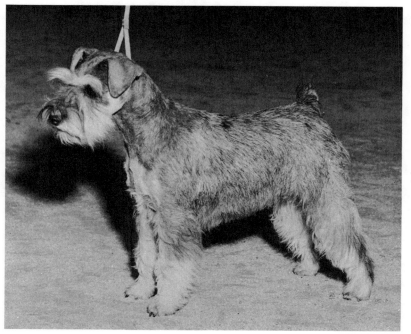

English Ch. Gosmore Trump Card, owned by Mrs. A. Dallison. Photo by C. M. Cooke & Son.

these characteristics, while keeping the ideal size, that the Miniature Schnauzer became a stable breed.

The first Miniatures were reported in Germany in 1899, in Swabia, which is considered the most important breeding area. Three foundation sires are the ancestors of practically all of today's Miniature Schnauzers. They are Peter v Westerberg (1902), bred in Munich; Prinz v Rheinstein (1903), bred in Frankfort; and Lord (1904), who was bred by George Reihl. These early dogs had the most desired qualities and were much in demand as studs.

Some of the most famous kennels were found in Germany. The Abbagamba was noted for its blacks, and Baltischort for its dogs who were a bit larger and had a reddish color. One of the early American kennels was the Marienhof, which bred Miniatures in dark mixed colors.

The modern Miniature Schnauzer is a mixture of Poodle, Spitz, Affenpinscher, and several other breeds, some of which are shrouded

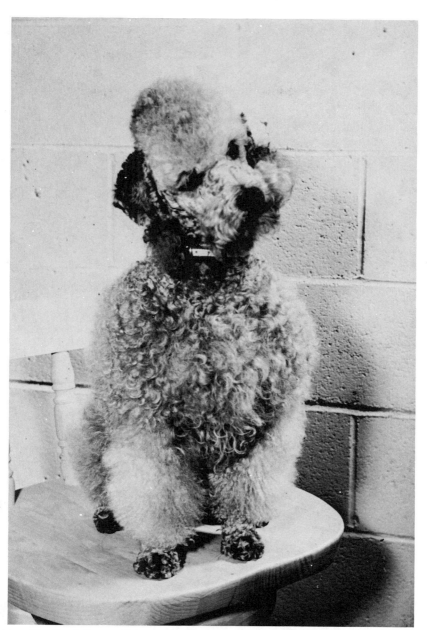

The Poodle is one of the ancestors of the modern day Miniature Schnauzer.

The Affenpinscher was used to get the diminutive size of the Miniature Schnauzer.

in mystery. Does this sound as if your alert, intelligent, well-bred pet is a mongrel? Of course not! All dogs began as mixtures and were gradually sorted out. At first, dogs were bred for utility—what they could do to help the hunter, farmer, herder. Breeders tried, by hit or miss efforts, to duplicate desirable traits and breed out poor qualities. A dog which caught someone's fancy was bred in an attempt to reproduce similar dogs. Indeed, few people could resist the Miniature Schnauzer's sparkling eyes shadowed by shaggy eyebrows, his appealing face framed by whiskers and beard, and, most important in a family dog, his amiable temperament. Today, modern breeders, with their knowledge of heredity and complete records of each dog's ancestors, can breed scientifically for better and finer dogs.

As soon as the Miniature Schnauzer was recognized, only purebred dogs were mated; we now have almost complete records from the first important sires and dams on down to today's descendants.

English Ch. Deltone Delaware, owned by R. P. Newman. Photo by C. M. Cooke & Son.

English Ch. Deltone Delsanta Barbara, owned by Mrs. M. B. C. Hardy. Photo by C. M. Cooke & Son.

FOREIGN HISTORY

Germany

The Miniature Schnauzer originated in Germany and continues to be a popular breed there. This dog, however, is bred throughout the world, something of which not all breeds can boast.

The Schnauzers appeared in the 1890's, and at the Third International Dog Show, held in Hanover, three Wire-haired Pinschers won prizes; "Schnauzer," "Betti," and "Anni." There were 93 Schnauzers shown in the first specialty show in 1890. The first Miniature champion was Jocco-Firlda, shown in 1899 in Germany.

Other Countries

Many other countries imported the Miniature, and he quickly found a place in everyone's heart. Clubs were formed by many enthusiasts. Although the Miniature Schnauzer is of Terrier stock

English Ch. Wilkern Tony from America, owned by Mrs. J. Creasy. Photo by C. M. Cooke & Son.

and known as a ratter, he cannot hunt other small animals because of his size, and cannot be compared to the British Terriers. He is classed as a Terrier in America, but not in Germany or England.

MODERN HISTORY OF THE MINIATURE SCHNAUZER

Miniature Schnauzers were originally considered part of the Pinscher class. Later the Pinschers branched off into smooth-haired (Pinschers) and wire-haired (Schnauzers), and still later the Miniature Schnauzer branch was formed. The Wire-haired Terrier may have been used originally as a ratter. Indeed, he is known by several names, including Ratter and Ratcatcher.

Such activities were necessary in many places where sanitation did not exist. But today it is doubtful whether many Miniature Schnauzers are used for such purposes. Although he can be used on

English Ch. Deltone Deldomingo, owned by Mrs. D. Crowe. Photo by C. M. Cooke & Son.

English Ch. Dondeau Haphazard, owned by H. D. P. Becker. Photo by C. M. Cooke & Son.

Canadian Ch. Rosehill Pocono Avenger is owned by Wm. A. Fillingham. Avenger was bred by Mrs. Hugh Simpson. Sire, Canadian and American Ch. Jonaire Pocono Gladiator; dam, Wee-Mites Donny Dale Mona Lisa. He is shown being handled by Mr. Fillingham.

the farm or in the stable, today he is most often found in the home, an alert guardian of the home and a loyal companion to the family. Because these dogs are easy to care for, eat very little, and enjoy the company of people, they have become known as ideal family dogs, ready to guard hearth and home, ready to play, and ready to compete in the show ring.

THE MINIATURE SCHNAUZER IN AMERICA

The Miniature Schnauzer arrived in America in 1923. Four dogs, the champion Amsel v d Cyriaksburg, her two daughters, and a male came to a small railway station near Boston in a wicker basket. You can imagine the sensation caused among the proper Bostonians because of the dogs' bearded, bewhiskered "schnauzers" and snapping dark eyes, peering at their new home from within the basket. Unfortunately, the male died, and another was sent from Germany, Mach v d Godl Bachohe, with the agreement that he would be sent

A Miniature Schnauzer in steady show pose. Photo by Al Barry of Three Lions, Inc.

Ch. Dorem Favorite (as a puppy) with his feline pal. Photo by Tassone Studio.

back in two years. Germany did not want to lose one of her valuable studs for long.

Amsel was the first Miniature to be shown in America, but the breed, as yet, was not recognized here. At the first Boston show she attended, the judge, so the story goes, tested for temperament—by using his cane!—and Amsel broke her leash. Despite this show of "temperament," she managed to win third prize.

After an extended dispute, the breed was recognized by the American Kennel Club (AKC) in 1926. The first specialty show was held in 1927 and 27 dogs were shown. One of the early champions was named "Moses Taylor." The name alone caused a stir, as most dogs have somewhat more dignified names. He was named after an old man who loved dogs and tended the stables on the farm where the Miniature was born. (Amsel v d Cyriaksburg was known here as "Old Betty," rather than by her more formal name.) Perhaps it is impossible to call these little fellows by such long names. We just recently saw in a show a Miniature Schnauzer whose name was "Charlie Brown."

As in Germany, a combined Schnauzer club sponsored all the Schnauzer types for a while, but in 1933 a separate Miniature

Ch. Jonaire Pocono Rock 'n Roll, bred and owned by Jonaire Kennels. Sire, Ch. Jonaire Pocono High Life; dam, Jonaire Benrook Romance. Rock 'n Roll, is the sire of six champions. Photo by Evelyn M. Shafer.

Schnauzer Club was founded, headed by Mrs. Isaac W. Jeanes. One of Mrs. Jeanes's dogs, Ch. Urian Thuringia, imported from Germany, was twice winner at Westminster.

CHARACTERISTICS WHICH HISTORY BRED

In later chapters the physical and mental characteristics of the Miniature Schnauzer will be discussed in detail. But one thing we must note: breeds of dogs didn't just grow like Topsy. Dog owners liked certain types of dogs for certain reasons and because of this, purebreds were encouraged. In this way they could be assured of traits and appearance. The first Terriers were used as ratters, but it is doubtful that our modern Schnauzers will spend much time hunting mice and rats. The Schnauzer's current appeal is his size, attractive coat, whiskery muzzle and alert, friendly, and intelligent disposition.

Once the size of the Miniature was stable, breeders tried to keep their dogs within the standard heights. The pepper-and-salt coat, much desired, is maintained with care, for this type of coloration is difficult to keep without good breeding practice. These and the other physical features are sought after, and scrupulous breeders are careful to retain them.

Most people want an alert and gentle dog. The Miniature is a guardian of home and family, but most of all he is a people-dog. He prefers people to other dogs, a home to a kennel, and his family above all. Indeed, he is happiest if he can follow someone through the house all day long, investigating shoes and slippers, discarded toys, and bits of food. He is a perfect apartment dweller, needing little exercise area and space.

Ch. Fraser's Fortune Hunter was bred and is owned by William and Veronica Fraser. Fortune Hunter is shown being handled by R. Stephen Shaw as Mrs. Paul M. Silvernail, judge, looks on. Photo by Evelyn M. Shafer.

Chapter II
Description

When you first went out looking for a dog, did you know that you wanted a Miniature Schnauzer?

Many people see a dog in a store window, and he is such a cute puppy that they immediately dash off and buy one just like him, or even buy that "doggie in the window."

Others come to like a dog they see in someone's home and ask where they can get a similar one. Or, if one of the dogs in the neighborhood has a litter of puppies, you will often see some of her children in nearby houses (even though some people prefer to send their look-alikes to other areas).

Still others, scientific in their selection of a dog, go to the library and look up different breeds of dogs, or write to the American Kennel Club for advice and information. Or they may find their dog through the magazines or newspapers which advertise puppies for sale.

No matter how you obtained your Miniature Schnauzer, we know that you were careful in your selection. There is no substitute for the reputable kennel and breeder. If you are aware of the AKC standards for your purebred dog and reject those dogs which are obviously below par, you will encourage breeders to use care in breeding, thereby enhancing the breed. Certainly, if you plan to mate your dog, you should be familiar with the standard in order to select a proper dog or bitch for your pet.

The Miniature Schnauzer has some very special qualities, and you should know what your dog is like, temperamentally and physically.

The Miniature Schnauzer is a miniature dog who is more of a "small dog" than a miniature in the usual sense. His stocky appearance and alert manner make him seem bigger than he really is. Indeed, he behaves as if he were 12 feet tall, not 12 inches. This dog is constantly on the alert in the household, always aware of his "family," his master or mistress, his responsibilities as a house dog and companion. When you see him, with his bright sparkling eyes, guarding the baby carriage or menacing the neighborhood cat, you can see that this is (as one author has said) "a small dog with a big personality." He has one of the most attractive temperaments in dogdom, which helps to account for his growing popularity.

For all his size, the Schnauzer is a rugged dog, up to the rigors of the barn and stable, but equally at home at the AKC show where his beauty and elegance, his handsome coat and attractive features, have earned him many honors. Breeders encourage alertness and intelligence, and, as a result, these dogs make excellent home guardians and companions.

Miniature Schnauzers should have an alert expression.

AKC STANDARDS

The American Kennel Club sets the standards for all breeds of pedigreed dogs in America. No dog can be the complete ideal, but show winners are generally those dogs which come closest to the ideal. If you are buying a dog for show purposes, it is wise to check the points you need. Even if you just want a dog for the home, you may still want to purchase a dog which conforms closely to the standards, for some day you may wish to have a litter. Selecting your dog carefully also discourages those unscrupulous breeders who turn out dogs with little regard for the quality of the breed.

Ch. Melmar's Livewire poses with owner Ann W. Kaeppler, left, as judge Thomas Keator looks on. Livewire was bred by Virginia Schultz. Photo by Wm. Brown.

Ch. Yankee Pride Colonel Stump is shown being handled by Tom Gately as General McKinley, judge, presents Westminster Best of Breed award. The champion is the sire of eight champions and was bred by Peter Babisch. He is owned by Mrs. Joseph Sailer. Photo by Evelyn M. Shafer.

A *fault* is a departure from the ideal. It is not enough to disqualify a dog from the show ring, but it hurts his chances of winning.

A *disqualifying fault* disqualifies a dog from showing. It is of a more serious nature than a fault.

The standards for the Miniature Schnauzer follow. If you wish more information you can write the Secretary of the American Miniature Schnauzer Club.

General Appearance

The Miniature Schnauzer is a robust, active dog of Terrier type, resembling his larger cousin, the Standard Schnauzer, in general appearance. He has an alert, active disposition. He is sturdily built, nearly square in proportion of body length to height, with plenty of bone, and without any suggestion of toyishness.

Lila Jones demonstrates the proper way of picking up a Miniature Schnauzer.

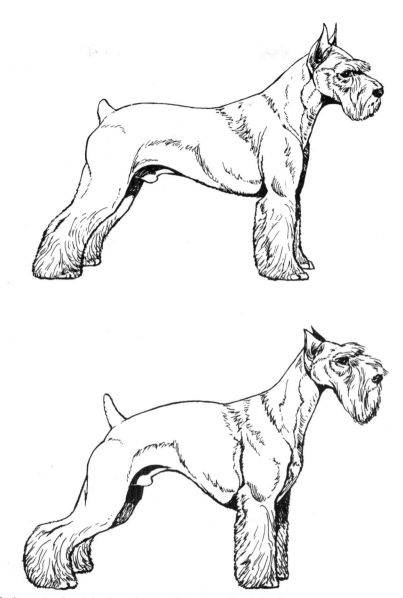

Faults to be found in the Miniature Schnauzer: (top) Ears cropped too long. Short in muzzle. Lacks whiskers. Short, heavy in neck. Shoulders set too far forward. Soft back. Round croup. Too long in loin. Pasterns soft. Lacks depth of chest. Too long in body. Lacks hindquarter angulation. Not enough bend in stifle. Bottom illustration: Roached back. Ears set too low. Neck lacks crest. Tail cut too long. Too much tuck-up. Forechest too prominent. Overangulated. Arched in loin.

Head

Strong and rectangular, its width diminishing slightly from ears to eyes, and again to the tip of the nose. The forehead is unwrinkled. The top skull is flat and fairly long. The foreface is parallel to the top skull, with a slight stop; it is at least as long as the top skull. The muzzle is strong in proportion to the skull; it ends in a moderately blunt manner, with thick whiskers, which accentuate the rectangular shape of the head.

Teeth

The teeth meet in a scissors bite. That is, the upper front teeth overlap the lower front teeth in such a manner that the inner surface of the upper incisors barely touches the outer surface of the lower incisors when the mouth is closed.

Eyes

Small, dark brown and deep-set. They are oval in appearance and keen in expression.

Ears

When cropped, the ears are identical in shape and length, with pointed tips. They are in balance with the head and not exaggerated

The thick whiskers should be combed to accentuate the shape of the head. Special dog combs are available at your pet shop.

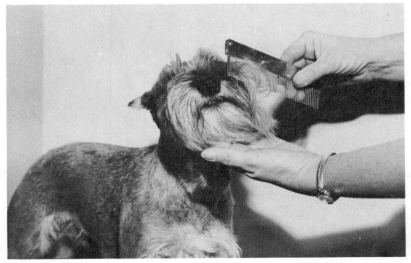

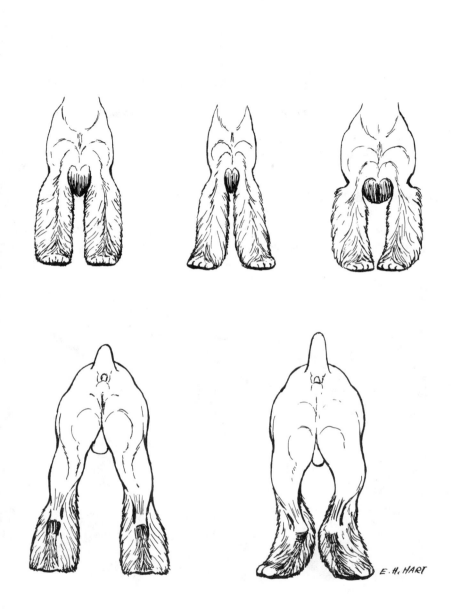

Top row, from left to right: excellent front; too narrow, fiddle front, pinched elbows; too broad, loaded shoulders, out at elbows, toes in. Bottom: an excellent rear; poor rear, being cowhocked and the tail was docked too long.

in length. They are set high on the skull and carried perpendicularly at the inner edges, with as little "bell" as possible along the outer edges. When uncropped the ears are small and v-shaped, folding close to the skull.

Neck

Strong and well arched, blending into the shoulders, and with the skin fitting tightly at the throat.

Body

Short and deep, with the brisket extending at least to the elbows. Ribs are well sprung and deep, extending well back to a short loin. The underbody does not present a tucked-up appearance at the flank. The topline is straight; it declines slightly from the withers

Ch. Magic of Sparks is shown being handled by Thomas Gately as judge Richard Kerns presents Best of Breed award. The champion was bred by Mrs. J. M. Deaver. He is owned by Peter Babisch. Photo by Wm. Brown.

to the base of the tail. The over-all length from chest to stern bone equals the height at the withers.

Forequarters

The forequarters have flat, somewhat sloping shoulders and high withers. Forelegs are straight and parallel when viewed from all sides. They have strong pasterns and good bone. They are separated by a fairly deep brisket which precludes a pinched front. The elbows are close, and the ribs spread gradually from the first rib so as to allow for the elbows to move close to the body.

Hindquarters

The hindquarters have strongly muscled, slanting thighs; they are well bent at the stifles and straight from hock to so-called heel. There is sufficient angulation so that, in stance, the hocks extend beyond the tail. The hindquarters never appear overbuilt or higher than the shoulders.

Feet

Short and round (cat-feet) with thick, black pads. The toes are arched and compact.

Movement

The trot is the gait at which movement is judged. When approaching, the forelegs, with elbows close to the body, move straight forward, neither too close nor too far apart. Going away, the hind legs are straight and travel in the same planes as the forelegs.

Note: It is generally accepted that when a full trot is achieved, the rear legs continue to move in the same planes as the forelegs, but a very slight inward inclination will occur. It begins at the point of the shoulder in front and at the hip joint in the rear. Viewed from the front or rear, the legs are straight from these points to the pads. The degree of inward inclination is almost imperceptible in a Miniature Schnauzer that has correct movement. It does not justify moving close, toe-ing in, crossing, or moving at the elbows.

Viewed from the side, the forelegs have good reach, while the hind legs have strong drive, with good pick-up of hocks. The feet turn neither inward nor outward.

Tail

Set high and carried erect. It is docked only long enough to be clearly visible over the topline of the body when the dog is in proper length of coat.

Coat

Double, with hard, wiry, outer coat and close undercoat. Head, neck and body coat must be plucked. When in show condition the body coat should be of sufficient length to determine texture. Close covering on neck, ears and skull. Furnishings are fairly thick but not silky.

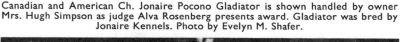

Canadian and American Ch. Jonaire Pocono Gladiator is shown handled by owner Mrs. Hugh Simpson as judge Alva Rosenberg presents award. Gladiator was bred by Jonaire Kennels. Photo by Evelyn M. Shafer.

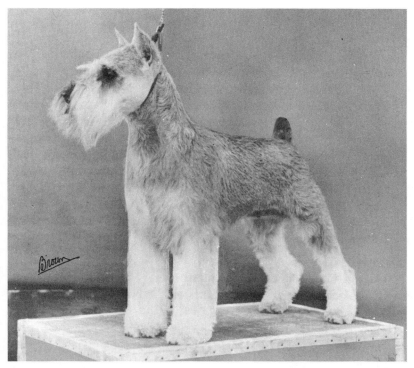

Ch. Dorem Originality was bred and is owned by Dorem Kennels. Photo by Wm. Brown.

Size

From 12 to 14 inches. Ideal size 13½ inches. (*See disqualifications.*)

Color

The recognized colors are salt and pepper, black and silver, and solid black. The typical color is salt and pepper in shades of gray; tan shading is permissible. The salt and pepper mixture fades out to light gray or silver white in the eyebrows, whiskers, cheeks, under throat, across chest, under tail, leg furnishings, under body, and inside legs. The light under-body hair is not to rise higher on the sides of the body than the front elbows.

The black and silvers follow the same pattern as the salt and peppers. The entire salt-and-pepper section must be black.

Black is the only solid color allowed. It must be a true black with no gray hairs and no brown tinge except where the whiskers may have become discolored. A small white spot on the chest is permitted.

Faults

Type: Toyishness, raciness, or coarseness.

Structure: Head coarse and cheeky. Chest too broad or shallow in brisket. Tail set low. Sway or roach back. Bowed or cowhocked hindquarters. Loose elbows.

Action: Sidegaiting. Paddling in front, or high hackney knee action. Weak hind action.

Coat: Too soft or too smooth and slick in appearance.

Temperament: Shyness or viciousness.

Bite: Undershot or overshot jaw. Level bite.

Eyes: Light and/or large and prominent in appearance.

Disqualifications

Dogs or bitches under 12 inches or over 14 inches.

Color solid white or white patches on the body.

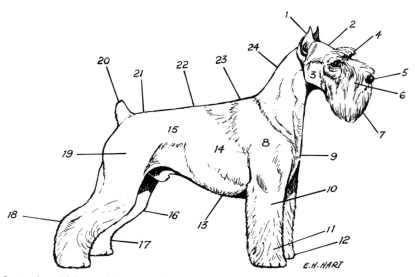

Parts of a Miniature Schnauzer: 1. Ears. 2. Skull. 3. Cheek. 4. Eyebrows. 5. Nose. 6. Muzzle. 7. Whiskers. 8. Shoulder. 9. Front. 10. Front leg. 11. Pastern. 12. Front feet. 13. Chest. 14. Ribs. 15. Loin. 16. Stifle. 17. Metatarsus. 18. Hock. 19. Thigh. 20. Tail or stern. 21. Croup. 22. Back. 23. Withers. 24. Neck.

Chapter III
Heredity

INTRODUCTION

Once upon a time there was a monk named Gregor Johann Mendel. And this monk had a pea patch. After some time he noticed that he could predict the appearance of his peas. He then began certain cross-breeding experiments and found that he could grow green peas or yellow peas, wrinkled peas or smooth peas, tall pea plants and short pea plants. From this ordinary pea garden, he produced an extraordinary science—genetics. Mendel experimented with his peas and evolved the early theories of inheritance which so changed the course of biology, agriculture, medicine, and other related sciences. Of course, theories of heredity have progressed far beyond anything Mendel could imagine, but it was his early experiments, unnoticed for many years, which touched off the revolution in the natural sciences.

Animal breeders were quick to use these theories in scientific breeding of purebred stock. Indeed, it is likely that many of them practiced scientific breeding without knowledge of scientific heredity. They bred like to like, bred dogs with favorable characteristics to obtain these traits in litters, and kept some records of bloodlines for mating purposes. They crossbred different types of dogs to encourage new traits. If they did not know just what it was that transmitted the desired features, they did know that somehow they were passed on to the young.

Good kennel management knows, however, that it is not enough to attend to heredity—to match up genes and chromosomes. This only transmits the raw material from dog to dog. The environment must

Ch. Miss Maxine of Crestwood Park is shown being handled by Tom Gately as General McKinley, judge, presents award. Sire, Ch. Yankee Pride Colonel Stump; dam, Ch. Sparkes Exotic. Breeder is Mrs. J. M. Deaver. Owners are Mrs. Aaron Salkowitz and J. M. Deaver. Photo by Wm. Brown.

also be proper. No matter how beautiful a dog's coat *could* be, all his careful breeding will be lost if he isn't groomed and fed properly. Therefore, modern breeders take advantage of modern science to breed scientifically, and then take care of the dogs which result from these litters.

THE THEORY OF INHERITANCE

There are many complex factors in inheritance, and modern geneticists are discovering more every day. Many things can influence the dog's breeding—but no outside interference, with the exception of accidental mutation, can change his genetic structure.

In every living thing we find two types of cells—soma and germ. The somatic cells make up every part of the organism but one—the germ plasm, which contains the germ cells. The germ plasm is the thin thread of our existence. Everything alive, from the lowliest amoeba to the dog and to man himself is dependent on germ plasm to perpetuate his kind.

Jonaire Pocono TV Girl, a salt and pepper female, takes best local dog award at Clearwater, Fla. show. Sire, Ch. Jonaire Pocono Reveille; dam, Torni's Grandioso. Shown from left to right are Melbourne Downing, judge, and a handler and club official. Photo by Evelyn M. Shafer.

Germ plasm in mammals is found in the sperm of the male and eggs of the female. This substance contains tiny chemical entities called genes. Genes or groups of genes control the form and development of specific physical and mental characteristics. It may take several genes or combinations of genes to produce a certain appearance. For example, any number of genes may control the look of your dog's coat. There are genes to determine color, texture, length, and curliness (or lack of it). All of these factors can act together to produce the pepper-and-salt wire-haired Miniature Schnauzer.

The geneticist tells us that all the genes are found in every cell of the animal: in pairs everywhere but in the germ plasm. Even though every cell (other than germ plasm) has a specialized function—skin, muscles, heart, eye, etc.—the nucleus still has within it the genetic "fingerprint" of the complete animal.

When the somatic cells are dividing and redividing during the formation of the new animal, they divide so that each gene divides in

Left, Canadian Ch. Rosehill Poco's Impression; right, Canadian Ch. Flintrock's Cobby of Rosehill. Both dogs were sired by Canadian and American Ch. Jonaire Pocono Gladiator, and were bred and are owned by Mrs. Hugh Simpson.

Miniature Schnauzer puppies sired by Canadian and American Ch. Jonaire Pocono Gladiator. The dam was Jonaire Pocono Poppy Seed. Owner, James Simpson.

half. Thus each somatic cell receives the same pair of genes. The germ plasm cells divide differently. They divide to form more cells, but each pair of genes divides in half (one-half the pair)—either one gene of the pair or the other to each new cell. When the egg and the sperm, each made up of the special germ cells with only half the normal number of genes, unite, the genes again become paired. Each new individual inherits half his genes from each parent, but we cannot tell which half until after he has been born, although we can determine what kinds of characteristics he will inherit from the appearance and genetic make-up of his parents. Since many different combinations are possible, he will inherit characteristics different from those of his brothers and sisters—in fact, each individual is unique unto himself, although he will resemble his species closely.

The important thing to remember is that each characteristic is determined by a pair of genes. How does this work? Why will two black dogs, mated, produce a litter of all black dogs, or litters with pepper-and-salt or black-and-silver?

Ch. Jonaire Pocono Reveille was sired by Ch. Wilkern Reveille. Dam, Jonaire Pocono Priscilla. The salt and pepper male was bred and is owned by Jonaire Kennels. Photo by Evelyn M. Shafer.

There are two types of genes—dominant and recessive. The dominant is the "stronger," you might say, and whenever it is present it overshadows the recessive or "weaker" gene. You can have a pair consisting of two dominant genes (purebred), two recessive genes (purebred), or a dominant and a recessive gene (hybrid). The recessive gene can show only if both the genes are recessive. But whenever one of the pair is a dominant gene, that characteristic will be the dominant one, although the recessive may show up some time later in another litter.

Let us say that **"B"** represents the dominant black color of the Miniature Schnauzer coat color, and that **"ps"** represents pepper-and-salt, which is recessive in Miniatures. Each dog has two genes, one from each parent, for his coat color. Since black is dominant over pepper-and-salt, whenever there is a **B** gene, the dog will be black. If the dog inherits a **B** gene from his father and a **B** gene from his mother he will be black, and will pass only black genes to his children. But if the father with his **BB** genes mates with a bitch with **ps-ps** genetic makeup (a pepper-and-salt color), the children will be black but will be capable of transmitting pepper-and-salt color genes. This means that if one of these children mates with a Miniature Schnauzer with a **"ps"** gene, pepper-and-salt *can* appear in *his* children. Simple listings of the combinations possible can enable any dog owner to see all the possible results of successive matings. It is by use of these Mendelian relations that the dog breeders control the quality of their dogs. Practically, it is difficult to see these effects when you produce only a litter or two, but the

Ch. Jonaire Pocono High Life is sire of four champions and was bred and is owned by Jonaire Kennels. Sire, Ch. Benrook Buckaroo; dam, Ch. Winsome High Style. Photo by Wm. Brown.

following variations are possible. These variations become very real when many litters are produced.

1. Two pure blacks mated will produce only purebred black dogs:
   BB x **BB** = **BB, BB, BB, BB.**
2. Two purebred pepper-and-salts when mated will produce only pepper-and-salt (recessive) coated dogs:
   ps-ps x **ps-ps** = **ps-ps, ps-ps, ps-ps, ps-ps.**
3. Two hybrids will produce some hybrids and some purebred dogs in the following ratios:
   B-ps x **B-ps** = **BB, B-ps, B-ps, ps-ps.**
4. A hybrid black and a purebred black will produce some purebred and some hybrid dogs, but they will all be black in appearance:
   BB x **B-ps** = **BB, B-ps, BB, B-ps.**

One way of illustrating how the gene theory works are boxes like the ones below:

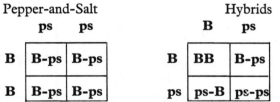

Purebred Black and
Pepper-and-Salt

	ps	ps
B	B-ps	B-ps
B	B-ps	B-ps

Hybrids

	B	ps
B	BB	B-ps
ps	ps-B	ps-ps

Of course, in any single mating these expectations may not be realized, but once you have had many matings and litters you will see the patterns coming up. Since this theory is known, you need not take any chances. You can study the pedigrees and bloodlines of both male and female and mate dogs which have characteristics you want. If you want pepper-and-salt Miniature Schnauzers and you know the color is recessive, you must either mate purebred pepper-and-salts (**ps-ps** x **ps-ps**) or hybrids (**B-ps** x **B-ps**), or hybrid and purebred (**ps-ps** x **B-ps**). In the first case you can be sure of the color, but in the second and third case there is a chance you will obtain some blacks.

Many people speak of a dog's bloodlines as if blood had something to do with inheritance. This is not true. We should more properly talk of "gene lines," for blood itself has nothing to do with inheritance. It is only one physical factor determined by the genes.

People once thought that influences on the pregnant mother would mark the puppies. We even know of people who still believe that if

52

Fraser's Jigger O' Jin is owned by Raymond Ranolde. He was bred by William and Veronica Fraser. Photo by Tri-county Photo Service.

the mother listens to music while pregnant, for example, that their child will have musical ability. Musical ability may run in the family (genes again), but this has nothing to do with playing the radio loudly during pregnancy.

MUTATIONS

This brings us to the problem of changes in types. There are persons who believe that if they clip the hair of their dog before the dog is mated, his puppies will have shorter coats. This is utter non-sense, as you can see from the explanation above. The length of a dog's coat is determined by his genetic makeup. If the breeder has been striving for shorter coats he can, using scientific methods, mate dogs who through chance have coats which are shorter than average. Inbreeding and line-breeding will then fix this characteristic, and dogs will be born with shorter coats.

Occasionally there is a mutation in a breed. Genes are not immune to accident. Changes may come about chemically or from radiation

Provide a whelping box in an out-of-the-way corner for your expectant Miniature Schnauzer. Photo by Al Barry of Three Lions, Inc.

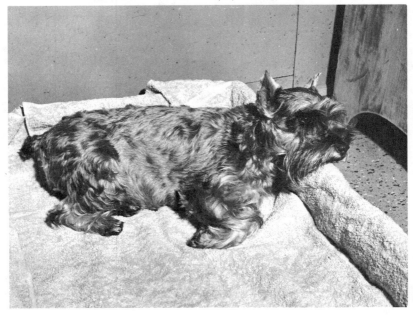

Six puppies is a fairly large litter for a Miniature Schnauzer bitch. Photo by Al Barry of Three Lions, Inc.

(such as X-rays or nuclear particles) or some mixup in the germ plasm. Sometimes chromosomes cross over, and this changes the genetic makeup. These changes are sudden and quite rare. If the breeder wishes to keep one of these mutant changes he can try to duplicate it with breeding, but most mutations are downward on the evolutionary scale; only rarely is one an improvement.

WAYS OF BREEDING

Using the knowledge of genetics or the old-time selective breeding, kennels are able to produce puppies which are almost perfect examples of their type. There are several ways of achieving this: inbreeding, line-breeding, out-breeding, or cross-breeding.

Inbreeding: You occasionally hear of "overbred" dogs. People will complain that too much inbreeding causes a dog to be temperamental or spoiled. Inbreeding itself doesn't cause this, but *sloppy* inbreeding does. Unfortunately, a few breeders are concerned only with how the puppy looks, not how he acts. And so they breed for beauty only. If they ignore the fact that both parents were difficult

Canadian and American Ch. Jonaire Pocono Gladiator sits in the lap of W. J. Maniotld.

dogs, or overly sensitive or temperamental, or nervous (*tendencies* toward mental characteristics can be inherited), and mate them because they are perfect specimens of their type, you may very well get a litter of overbred, oversensitive dogs.

Inbreeding means doubling up on genes, by mating dogs in the same immediate family, such as father to daughter or mother to son, or brother to sister.

If the father has a black coat and the daughter has a black coat, even if one carries the recessive pepper-and-salt gene, all the dogs will be black and there will be quite a few with **BB** as genetic makeup. Then, if you were to mate the father with one of his granddaughters, you would add to the purebred black dogs. Brother and sister can also be mated very successfully. Of course, if bad characteristics show up, you immediately stop mating this particular pair of dogs and their offspring.

Inbreeding among animals is an accepted thing, but it is done carefully. Today such inbreeding, or incest, is forbidden among humans in almost every society. In the past, tragic results occurred from inbreeding; for example, certain European royal families inherited hemophilia as a result of intermarriage.

Line-Breeding: Line-breeding is mating dogs fairly closely related, keeping within a family, avoiding very close relations. To establish a strain, dogs must be bred with a combination of inbreeding and line-breeding. All modern breeds are inbred and line-bred, as can be seen if you study their pedigrees.

Out-Breeding: Out-breeding is mating dogs very distantly related, or possibly not at all related, although they must be pedigreed dogs in the same breed for the litter to be registered.

Cross-Breeding: The thousands of mongrels you see are the result of cross-breeding, which is not done by breeders at all. However, there are times when it is valuable. In the case of the Miniature Schnauzer, it is known that the size of the breed was changed when a small standard Schnauzer was mated with the Affenpinscher—a

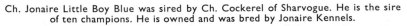

Ch. Jonaire Little Boy Blue was sired by Ch. Cockerel of Sharvogue. He is the sire of ten champions. He is owned and was bred by Jonaire Kennels.

miniature dog. This accounts for the Miniature's size. Early breeders, desiring this size, deliberately cross-bred the Schnauzer with the Affenpinscher.

HOW HEREDITY AFFECTS PHYSICAL CHARACTERISTICS AND BEHAVIOR

Scientists are still experimenting with animals to see just how an animal learns. Is a particular trait, such as scenting a trail, learned or inherited? The most we can say now is that certain tendencies run in families, and whether a pair of genes is responsible for this or it is learned through association is not yet clear. Psychologists do know that if they take a family of rats which are very good at finding their way through a maze, the children of the family will learn to find their way in the maze more quickly than rats from another, less talented, family. If you take one of the rats away from its family and put it with another family which is not as adept, it will not learn to get through the maze, but if you put it back with its own family it will learn more quickly than other rats might. Regardless of how a trait is acquired, family characteristics are most important, as dog breeders have discovered through their experience. Many examples are known.

Among all the bird-hunting breeds, the Spaniels are the only ones which are bred to keep their noses close to the ground, Hound fashion, when they hunt. Setters and Pointers hunt with heads high. In crosses of Cockers and Setters the puppies all hunt with heads up, like Setters. Even in crosses of Setters with Bloodhounds the progeny are useless as trailing dogs. When you see a Cocker hunt with head carried high, he probably has some inherited characteristics of English Setter in him.

Some of the smaller breeds are natural tree dogs, and many make squirrel dogs *par excellence*, a use to which only those with shorter coats can be put. Some Poodles tree almost as well as hunting dogs bred for this, and this aptitude is not so well recognized as it should be, although it is by squirrel hunters.

While most persons never give posing much thought, observant breeders can tell you how much easier it is to get certain dogs to pose as show dogs than others. There are many who will stand in a show pose when no hand is on or under them. This characteristic seems to run in families.

Fraser's Jeminy is a salt and pepper female owned and bred by William and Veronica Fraser. She is shown here handled by Veronica Fraser as judge Twyla Miller presents award. Photo by Wm. Brown.

Ch. Jonaire Pocono High Class is a salt and pepper female with an N.B.R. rating of 436.25. Sire, Ch. Benrook Buckaroo; dam, Ch. Winsome High Style. She was bred and is owned by Jonaire Kennels.

Miss Edna Dobbins handled Mankit's Elsa to a total of fourteen points. Breeder, Emanuel Miller. Mankit's Elsa is owned by Mrs. J. M. Deaver. Photo by Wm. Brown.

Gun-shyness also seems to run in families. Such dogs are also thunder-shy. It would appear best not to breed them, although it is possible to train these dogs so that they are not a total loss for hunting or retrieving.

The tendency to piddle is another characteristic which appears to be inherited. Unfortunately, it is often overlooked by breeders. There are too many dogs which are incontinent and panic when strangers or even their masters approach, and then wet. This is certainly most discouraging if your dog is a house dog and you want to preserve your rugs. It can be watched for and then eliminated by careful breeding.

All typical retrieving breeds love to retrieve, but there are strains in which there is no interest, and retrieving can be trained into these dogs only with great difficulty. On the other hand, you can often see a leashed city-bred dog, familiar only with sparrows and pigeons, get out in a field and display a natural instinct for the art of retrieving. Careful breeding will help to preserve the hunting breeds and keep them from losing these instincts.

Practice makes perfect in stacking for show, too. Photo by Al Barry of Three Lions, Inc.

A natural combination: a boy and a Miniature Schnauzer. Photo by Al Barry of Three Lions, Inc.

Natural retrievers seem to have an overpowering need to carry something around in their mouths. Some dogs can be taught more easily to get the paper or the mail, or even carry something in a bag. One dog we know came to visit and spent the entire afternoon carrying sticks of wood to his master on the patio. By the end of the day we had a considerable pile of winter firewood, and we promptly invited our friend to come back again soon with his dog to complete the job. Many retrievers will even resort to picking up stools and carrying them around. If you have some old tennis balls around you can discourage this habit.

Swimming is another characteristic that seems to be inherited although the natural tendency has to be encouraged by parent dogs which swim or owners who encourage swimming. Water-dog retrievers have to know how to swim, but there is great variation among families within breeds. If you want to hunt, and own a water retrieving dog, or live near water, you will want a dog with this characteristic.

The tendency to contract disease may be inherited. We know that certain tendencies run in human families, such as heart trouble and length of life. Back in the days when vaccines were not available and epidemics were rampant in animal families, it was seen that certain breeds did not have the same early symptoms of distemper as other dogs. Most dogs were found to have convulsions when the temperature first starts to rise, but Cockers and Poodles did not. Although mortality rates were the same, the symptoms differed.

Schnauzers were used once as ratters and guardians of the stable and barnyard. A dog engaged in such work must have acute sense of smell and agility too, as well as excellent hearing. If these characteristics run in families, it would be wise to mate dogs within the family and to breed out those that are not keen of ear and nose. In addition, now that the Miniature Schnauzer has become a favorite family dog,

Good temperament is inherited, too.

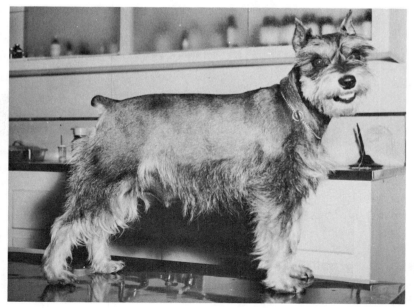

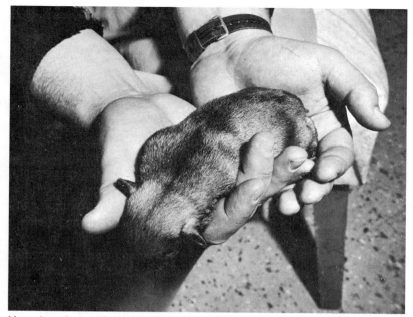

Note the coloring of this day-old puppy. He'll have a salt and pepper coat when he is mature. Photo by Al Barry of Three Lions, Inc.

those dog strains which show any signs of viciousness or lack of intelligence should be bred out as fast as possible.

There is obviously much to be learned in this fascinating field of inheritance. Modern science, which has expanded and complicated Mendel's simple ideas, still has far to go. We can predict the inheritance of physical characteristics such as color, shape, coat, skin, etc., although we cannot always be absolutely sure of the results. With so many factors to consider (such as color, size, coat, etc.), the possible variations are almost infinite in the more complex mammals. As for inheriting or acquiring mental characteristics such as temperament, hunting ability, and tendencies for diseases, there is considerable disagreement among animal psychologists, but the consensus appears to be that the tendency to learn these traits is most likely inherited, although the traits themselves must be taught in some fashion.

Chapter IV
Inherited Characteristics of the Miniature Schnauzer

The Mendelian theories of inheritance tell us how characteristics are passed from parents to children. But, as noted in Chapter III, the early experiments of Johann Mendel have been elaborated and modified by modern scientists. For an animal like the dog, many genetic factors may be responsible for any one characteristic.

COAT COLOR

How many factors influence your dog's coat? Combinations of genes determine whether your Miniature Schnauzer will have a coat that is all black, pepper-and-salt, or black-and-silver. One gene is responsible for the intensity of the black color: in a pepper-and-salt dog, too much black will result in a grayish appearance. Another single gene produces a solid color coat. Genes are responsible for the change of color in a puppy, or the even distribution of dark pigment over the coat. And in other breeds of dogs, genes produce the piebald effect and the "mask" around the face. As you can see, many genes, and consequently many factors, influence your dog's appearance; the breeder is faced with a myriad of choices. How careful he is and how well he chooses his dogs and their mates will show up in the quality of his dogs.

In charting the genetic makeup of the Miniature Schnauzer, the breeder knows that the all-black coat color is dominant over the pepper-and-salt coat. If he mates two all-black dogs, he will certainly have some black puppies, but if both the parents have genes in their backgrounds for pepper-and-salt coloration, this may appear in the children.

Pepper-and-salt coloration, which is very popular, is the result of a pattern called "agouti," consisting of hairs banded with color. The white hair shades to black at the tip. A reverse of this pattern, the chinchilla, which is occasionally seen, is created by hairs which shade from black to white at the tip. The exact shade of pepper-and-salt color depends on the amount of black pigment present.

The Miniature Schnauzer may become all black as a result of two different genetic factors. Black, as over-all coloration, is dominant over pepper-and-salt, and if one or both parents are black, some or all of the puppies will be black. Another reason for change in coloration from pepper-and-salt to all-black is the loss of the pattern factor which causes a loss of the shading from white to black in the hairs. This is a recessive trait and can be prevented by careful breeding.

Coloration in the Miniature Schnauzer is also influenced by another pattern factor. The all-black dog has no patches of color.

The two puppies at the right will probably mature into salt and peppers, while the one at the left will have a black coat.

In the pepper-and-salt dog, however, the coloring gradually fades out to light gray or silver-white in the eyebrows, whiskers, cheeks, areas under the tail and body, on the legs and inside the legs. Black-and-silver dogs are black except in the eyebrows, whiskers, etc., where they are silver or gray.

Another genetic factor is the reddish undercoat which some dogs have, an ancestral throwback.

TEXTURE

The texture and appearance of the wire-haired dog is one of his most popular qualities. Wire-hair is a mixture of tangled plus short-coated hair. Whiskers, eyebrows, and beard all result from this type of hair also. As a result of the attractive coat qualities, wire-haired dogs in the Terrier breed have become much more popular than other types of Terriers, so that only a few short-haired Terrier breeds are left. Wire-hair is dominant over smooth hair, so the quality is easy to maintain.

Scissors are used to trim the stockings of a Miniature Schnauzer. See your pet shop for proper shears, as well as other grooming equipment.

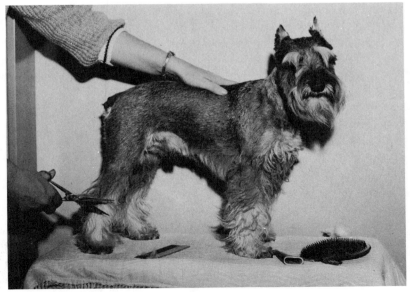

This Miniature Schnauzer's coat is ready for a trim and stripping. Should you feel that you are unprepared to do the job, take your dog to a pet shop where it will receive professional grooming.

SIZE

The AKC standards specify that Miniature Schnauzers should be 12 to 14 inches high, and 13½ inches is the ideal size. Bitches are usually a little smaller than males.

The size of a dog can determine his usefulness. One of the Miniature's advantages is his size. Small enough to fit into a small home or apartment, he is large enough to be fun. Very small toy dogs are sometimes just too small to fit in with active family life of a family which includes children. But the Miniature Schnauzer is large enough to hold his own. This has been one main problem of the Miniature Schnauzer breeder, to keep the Miniature from becoming a toy.

Since the Schnauzer is rarely used as a ratter any longer, his size is not a deterrent to utility.

TEMPERAMENT

As has been said, psychologists and geneticists are not sure whether certain traits of behavior are inherited or not, and this is still being investigated. We do know that the best of dogs (from a genetic standpoint) can be ruined by improper training and care. And a relatively unpromising dog can certainly become a faithful and loving pet if he is treated well.

The Miniature Schnauzer is primarily a family dog. He does not thrive in large kennels. He is a one-man dog (few dogs are not!) but he does love and protect other members of the family.

An outstanding characteristic of the Miniature Schnauzer is his intelligence. Most scientists and breeders believe that intelligence is inherited. One of your dog's ancestors was the Poodle, known for his superior intelligence, and this trait seems to have carried over to the Schnauzer.

It is easy to train Schnauzers as watchdogs, or to teach them such tricks as begging or "playing dead." As a watchdog, the Miniature knows no equal. He is alert, keen-sensed and hardy. While, because of his size, he may not be capable of attack (and it is not wise to train a dog to attack unless he is being used in some military or police work), he can effectively warn his masters of possible danger.

Photograph shows the size of a four-month-old Miniature Schnauzer compared to an adult rabbit.

A Miniature Schnauzer is definitely a family dog.

The Miniature Schnauzer is especially good with children. We remember a recent dog show when a group of children fell in love with a young Miniature Schnauzer. He had just come out of the ring, tense and excited from the strain of showing. Despite this, he welcomed the children and stood quietly while they patted him. When his owner led him off he looked wistfully back, hoping they would follow him. We should add here that children should be taught not to tease or hurt a dog while they are playing. We remember watching in horror as a small child practically pulled the ears off his family dog. The dog let out an occasional whimper and finally ran off, but he didn't so much as growl at his young master (and tormentor). This was certainly the case of a well-trained dog and a poorly-trained child.

APPEARANCE

The best way to judge a dog's appearance is to compare him with the AKC standard.

In physique the Miniature Schnauzer appears small but sturdy. His compact build and one-foot height are extremely attractive.

What most people like about the Miniature, however, is his attractive coloring and bewhiskered, bearded face. With his pepper-and-salt or black coat, bright eyes peering out from under bushy eyebrows and bearded and bewhiskered muzzle, he is hard to resist.

Early pictures show the Miniature somewhat under the influence of the Affenpinscher, but careful breeding has bred out the undesirable characteristics and kept the best. The purpose of the cross with the Affenpinscher was to obtain the Affenpinscher's size, not other traits, and it was important that the Schnauzer coloration and appearance be preserved with the new size. Black, the color of the Affenpinscher, does appear in the Miniature Schnauzer more

Miniature Schnauzers are small but sturdy dogs.

All puppies are cute, but Miniature Schnauzers fit into the scheme of all things.

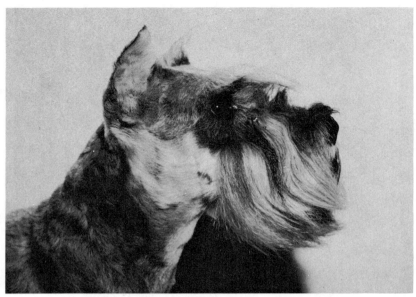

Photograph shows good head profile and ear crop.

Puppies are born with smooth coats.

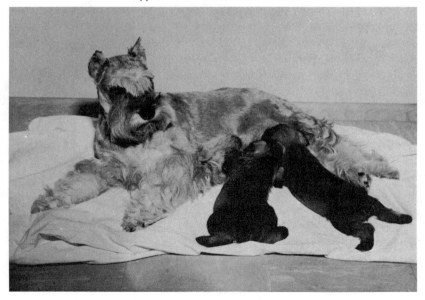

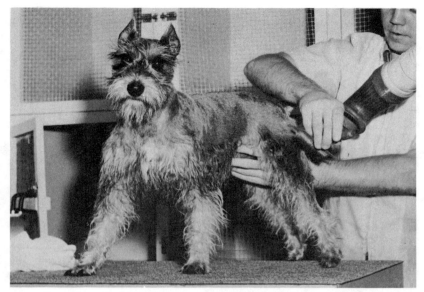

Grooming will add much to the appearance of your Miniature Schnauzer.

Note the difference in coat color.

Top dogs can go on to be show winners. Photo by Ludwig.

frequently as a result of the blend. Note also that the Affenpinscher, while not the same breed, has similar characteristics. A wire-haired dog of the Pinscher group, he is not too far removed from the wire-haired Schnauzer. Therefore it was not too hard to cross the two breeds and retain the most desirable features of both.

One of the things to note about the Miniature Schnauzer's appearance is that careful grooming will add much to his looks. Proper plucking and combing will keep the wire-haired coat from tangling and proper diet will maintain the tone of his coat and skin as well.

LIFE SPAN

Most dogs live to a ripe old age if given proper care. The Methuselahs of the dog world may reach 18 or 20 years of age, and 12 and 14 is about average. The Miniature Schnauzer, a sturdy active type, should have many years of useful life.

Chapter V
Reproduction

Would you like to raise a litter of puppies? Even if you purchased your pet with no intention of breeding, there may come a time when you would like to see its offspring. Or, as is often the case, despite all your precautions, someone has gotten into the barn and stolen the horse, and your dog is pregnant, the sire unknown.

Breeding raises many problems for the novice, and we suggest that you familiarize yourself with Chapter III, the principles of heredity, before you undertake to breed your dog for purebred puppies.

CONTRACTS

If you are planning a litter of purebreds, your best bet is to go to a professional kennel and arrange for a stud (male dog). Be prepared, however, for making contractual arrangements, and the authors believe that if large amounts of money or complicated arrangements are involved, you should have your lawyer check the contract. In general, there are two types of fees. Most kennels charge a fee for the use of a stud. This may vary from $25 to $200, depending on the dog. If the stud is a famous champion, the cost will be higher. The other type of contract is written so that the owner of the stud gets the pick of the litter. In this case, the breeder has first choice of a puppy or puppies. Be sure that all contingencies are spelled out. In most contracts, if your bitch fails to be impregnated the first time, you can rebreed her with the same dog when she is next in heat for no extra charge. This is called a *return service*.

Have your Miniature Schnauzers on leads when introducing them to each other as breeding partners.

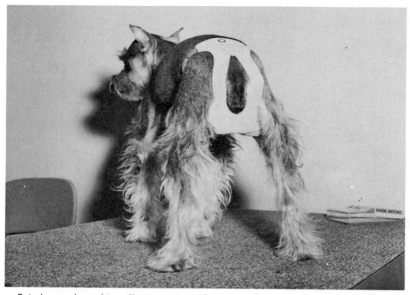

Britches such as this will protect your furniture while your female is in estrus.

THE BITCH

A little friend of ours always talks about when his dog is "heating", much to our amusement. But he does understand something about the reproductive process and we feel that this is important. This is an excellent way to explain to children, in as much or as little detail as you wish, the way dogs (and people) are "made." It is certainly far more reliable than the information picked up on street corners from uninformed children.

Dogs, like people, ovulate rhythmically, excepting that where humans ovulate 13 times a year, dogs only come into heat (i.e. ovulate) twice a year. All mammals have the same type of reproductive organs, and although they are not alike in appearance they work in the same manner.

REPRODUCTIVE ORGANS

The female ovaries are located in the abdomen, high behind the ribs. Each ovary is encircled by a capsule with a slit on one side.

The capsule is surrounded by spongy tissues known as the *fimbria*. Starting at the slit of each ovary are the *Fallopian tubes*, two tiny tubes which run a zigzag course over each capsule and terminate at the upper end of one of the branches of the Y-shaped *uterus*.

The eggs in the ovaries contain germ plasm, that unique bit of matter which determines your dog's inheritance and assures the continuance of the breed. When the eggs mature, they ripen in blister-like pockets which grow towards the surface of the ovaries. These pockets, called *follicles*, produce a follicular hormone which

Have the Miniature Schnauzer checked for internal parasites, and dewormed if necessary, before she is put to a stud.

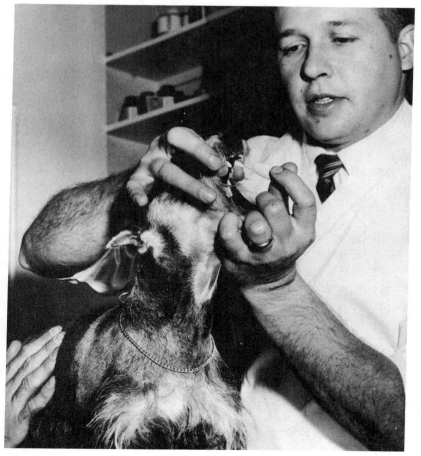

Never breed a pet-type Miniature Schnauzer.

prepares the uterus. The walls of the pockets are thin and eventually burst, liberating the eggs into the capsule surrounding the ovaries, and they move into the Fallopian tubes and are ready for fertilization. Your dog is "heating."

When copulation occurs (the mating of the bitch with the male dog), sperm are transferred from the male to the female and are moved up the uterus by the same sort of movement (peristalsis) that occurs in the intestines. Within a few minutes of tieing (mating) the sperm are already up in the uterus, through the tubes, and in the capsule surrounding the ovaries.

It takes many sperm to help fertilize one egg; the sperm has an enzyme which breaks down the egg's resistance until one sperm enters. Only one is needed for *fertilization*, and as soon as this sperm has entered the egg, the egg changes and becomes impervious to other sperm.

The eggs, fertilized or not, move down through the Fallopian tubes into the uterus and there, if fertilized, become attached to the uterine lining (endometrium) and grow. Oftentimes, they are not

After the female has been bred, take her for a quick walk around the block, but keep her on a leash.

fertilized in the capsule, but meet the sperm in their travels to the uterus and are fertilized and then nest in the uterus. The chromosomes in the egg and the sperm unite, making a complete set. The fertilized egg divides six times, each cell containing the same chromosomes, and at the sixth division one pair of cells are formed which become the germ plasm of the pup. The dividing cells form a hollow globe, which finally pulls in on one side, as if you let the air out of a hollow rubber ball and pushed one side of it in until it touched the other side. If you then squeezed the ball together until you made a canoe-shaped body, and continued squeezing until the two gunwales touched and stayed closed, you would duplicate the process of cell division in the egg.

By the twenty-second day the foetus (unborn puppy) is a very tiny object which is surrounded by protective coverings (the sac) and the placenta which is a band of flesh connecting the foetus with the uterus. At this point, if you put your thumb and fingers on each side of the bitch's belly, you will feel the tiny marble-like lumps which are puppies. These grow and by the twenty-fourth day they are larger and continue to grow until you can't distinguish the individual puppies, as the lumps are so soft. By this time, your dog, however, looks pregnant, as just a glance at her size will tell you.

Hold the bitch this way when having her bred.

Feed the bred bitch an adequate commercial diet to keep her in good health.

THE OVULATION CYCLE

As we have already said, ovulation is a rhythmic cycle occurring twice a year, about once every six months. Scientists believe that the changing length of the day is the chief influence inducing the cycle which makes the reproduction possible. As the days grow shorter in late summer and longer in late winter, most bitches come into heat.

This fact can be used to bring the bitch into heat artificially by the use of artificial light. If the length of her day is increased by light, one hour the first week, two the second, three the third, and four the fourth, she can be brought into heat by the end of the fourth week. Even shipping a bitch from one part of the country to the other, where the days have different lengths, can change her cycle. Be careful, therefore, if you move your dog from Maine to Georgia; you may find yourself with a bitch ready for mating.

A more certain method of bringing the bitch into heat artificially is the use of drugs such as stilbestrol, which encourages ovulation.

Select the stud that complements your bitch's type.

At a large kennels you will have many studs to select from.

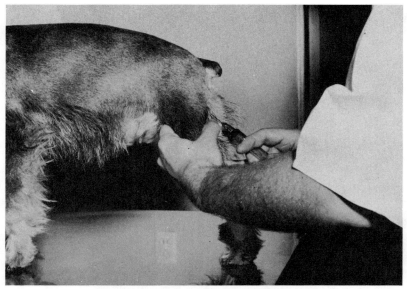
Stilbestrol can be given to encourage ovulation.

THE MATURE CYCLE

A female's cycle is made up of four parts; the *proestrum*, the *estrum*, the *anestrum*, and the *metestrum*. She will ovulate during a three-week period and the manner in which this occurs makes it possible for you to quickly get your dog under cover or plan for mating.

The first signs of ovulation, the period of *proestrum*, are an enlarged and swollen vulva and a bloody discharge. The follicles, which hold the eggs, are rupturing, and forming bloody plugs (pits) called blood bodies (*corpora hemorrhagica*) which soon change and secrete a hormone called the *luteal hormone*. The blood bodies become quite tough and are now called *luteal bodies*. This hormone brakes the mating cycle and at this point the dog enters the *estrum* period. Up to now she has not been interested in males. But they are interested in her! She is restless, her appetite may increase and she has the physical symptoms listed above. Now her vulva loses its firmness and within 36 hours becomes flabby and soft. The color of the discharge changes and becomes paler. By the second week your bitch is ready to accept the male and his advances. The eggs are not ready

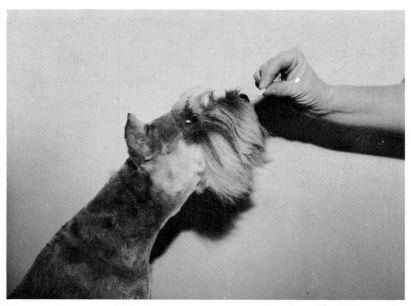

Once your bitch has been bred you can insure her continued good health by supplementing her diet with vitamins and minerals. Special preparations for dogs can be purchased at your pet shop.

for fertilization before the middle of the acceptance period, however, and since the sperm can only live about three days in the female, you should not mate her before the 10th day after the first signs of discharge, close to ovulation, either a day before or any time during the rest of the period of estrum.

The next two months are called the *anestrum* and the next three the *metestrum*, being the five month period when the bitch is not in heat. After this she's ready to begin again.

If you do not wish to mate your dog, you have only one problem—keeping her from getting pregnant. The careful dog owner will either send his dog to a kennel until ovulation is over, or keep the dog in the house and on a leash when outside. Even so, the male dogs will collect from all corners. It seems that the urine of a dog about to come into heat has a peculiar odor which attracts male dogs. Many dogs, when walked on the leash, are taken far from home so that the urine odor is not present around the house. If you live in an apartment, you can purchase a belt in the pet store which will protect your dog and also your rugs.

MATING THE MINIATURE SCHNAUZER BITCH

Suppose you have decided to have a litter of purebred pups. When and how should you arrange for this? Your dog matures at about 8 months or more. Some dogs, especially large breeds or toys, ovulate for the first time as late as twelve months or more. Are they ready for breeding? Some breeders say no, that they are not ready, are not mature enough to care for puppies. However, there are many compelling reasons for mating your dog as soon as you can. For one thing, it is easier for a young dog with flexible bones to bear her puppies than an older one. The puppies will be just as good as ones bred later on in life. The bitch can certainly take care of her puppies. Nature provides hormones to aid her. And if she seems awkward with the first litter, this is merely inexperience and she will improve with her next litters. Just think how most new mothers feel about their first child and how awkward each operation like bathing and dressing seems. By the second, things are much easier.

Another excellent reason for early breeding is preserving the blood lines. After all, many accidents can happen to dogs as they grow older and if you have bred your bitch and obtained a litter of puppies, you have sons and daughters to carry on the "family name." Many professional breeders breed early to ascertain which dogs are the best breeders.

When your dog is ready for breeding, be sure she is in good health. If your bitch is a virgin, you should have an experienced male dog. The virgin may be nervous or jumpy and an equally new stud will only make it worse. The experienced dog knows just what to do and is efficient and calm. Many people send their dog to the kennel and come and collect her when it is all over. But often your presence is required, especially if she is nervous. Generally, your dog is mated two or perhaps three times, once a day, and then sent home. You may have to help. If she refuses to permit copulation you will have to hold her up with your hand under her stomach. Once the two dogs are "tied," then the stud will be gently turned, and the period of copulation will last from several minutes to several hours. The reasons for this will be explained later, in the section on the male dog.

After mating it is advised that you keep the female quiet, and she may be serviced again the next day. Obviously, you must be sure that no other dogs get to her after this mating, for if she has not been impregnated the first time, you may end up with a litter of puppies, father unknown. If the mating has taken, you will become the proud owner of a litter of pups about 63 days later.

SPAYING

Suppose that you have a female dog and don't wish to mate her. You may not want to go through the bother and expense of kenneling her when she is in heat or the nuisance of the collection of amorous male dogs outside your door. A bitch can best be spayed before her first heat, at about five months. This is accomplished by a surgical operation called a hysterectomy, when the sexual organs are removed. Many people say that a spayed dog becomes fat and lazy,

Keep your Miniature Schnauzer bitch on a lead or in a secure kennel until her estrus is over.

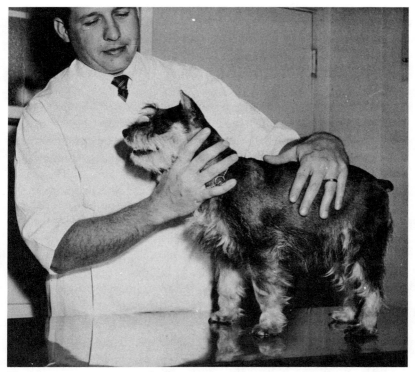

Should you never want your bitch to have puppies, you can have her spayed by a veterinarian.

but this need not be true. If you regulate your dog's diet and see that she gets enough exercise, she will probably remain fairly normal in size.

REPRODUCTION IN THE MALE

Most male dogs can be bred from about the age of a year until they are quite old. Some oldsters of 10 years or more have been known as perfectly fine studs. Handlers feel that a good stud can be mated several times a week for several weeks in succession, but then a rest is in order. Of course, his health must be maintained, the diet good, and condition tip-top. If you own a male and wish to mate him, perhaps for a puppy or two, you will find it more difficult. Most breeders have their own studs and are looking for females. But you may be fortunate to find a breeder or an individual with a female dog he wishes to mate to a dog of your male's characteristics. Again, be sure the contract is properly checked.

REPRODUCTIVE ORGANS

The sperm in the male dog are tiny bodies shaped like polliwogs. They are oval and flattish, with a tail about nine times the size of the body. Each sperm has half the necessary number of chromosomes. But there is one important difference between male sperm and female eggs. The male sperm determines the sex of the puppy. There are two different types of sex chromosomes in the sperm, one the **X** and the other the **Y**. The egg contains only **X** chromosomes. When **X** and **X** unite, the result is a female puppy, when the **X** and the **Y** unite, you have a male puppy.

The sperm are manufactured in the testicles by the germ plasm. The development of the dog's genitals follows a regular course as in other mammals. Before puberty, the testicles, which form inside the body, descend into a loose sac. They are attached to the peritoneum and grow down through the abdominal slits (known as rings) and drop into the sac, which is called the *scrotum*. The testicles are outside the body, as the warmth of the body can interfere with the manufacture of the sperm. But nature sees that they are protected against the weather and other dangers. When it is very cold a muscle pulls the testicles close to the body, and when warm weather comes, the muscle loosens so that the air can cool them.

If a dog's testicles fail to descend the condition is called *cryptorchidism*. Use of the hormone APL, administered by the veterinarian, can correct this condition, but it is considered hereditary and this might make your dog an unpopular stud. If only one testicle descends the condition is called *monorchidism* and the dog with no testicles (and no chance of fatherhood) is called an *anorchid*.

The dog's penis is unusual in that it contains a bone in the front part which aids the dog to achieve copulation. In addition, besides being capable of enlarging with blood, the penis also has an area which enlarges much more than the forepart does. When the male mates with a female dog, his penis swells and the bulbous part becomes at least three times the size of the rest of the penis. This prevents the penis from slipping out during copulation, at which time the dogs are "tied."

When tieing has occured, the semen is pumped in spurts into the vagina. Rhythmic waves which tighten and relax the vagina help also. Some males remain tied five minutes, others an hour or longer. But a five-minute tie can be just as satisfactory, as the semen have moved up through the uterus and tubes to the ovaries by that time.

MATING THE MINIATURE SCHNAUZER

If your dog is inexperienced, it is best to mate him when he is about a year old to an experienced female. You may have to push him towards her or even force him. Be sure that the bitch does not snap or bite at him. Occasionally, the dogs may have difficulty mating, especially if they are of different sizes. If you are not experienced, it is best to have the assistance of a knowledgeable handler. He will know all the tricks of the trade and insure a successful mating. The first two or three services are very important and unless they are properly handled, your dog may have trouble mating in the future.

After the first service, the dogs will be rested. If the male is young and not too successful the first time, the handler may let him try again in a few hours. For a new dog, it is best to have a bitch just coming into heat, so that by the time the male is more used to her and experienced, she will not have passed her ovulation period.

Will you injure your dog if you don't mate him? Or will he be oversexed if he is mated often? Most breeders say no. They do feel that it is unwise to start to mate your dog after he is four years old. By this time it is too late to accustom him to the problems of fatherhood. But most unpenned dogs will roam, and will react to the female in heat. If your dog is not kept penned, the chances are that he will find a stray female somewhere. If you wish your dog to be a good stud, it is wise not to let him roam. As you have seen, it is difficult to train the young male to be a good stud. Allow him to mate only with proper dogs, under proper conditions where there is little chance of injury, and he will retain his value as a stud. By keeping a record of your dog's offspring, you will be able to determine in advance what kind of puppies will result from matings with a particular type of bitch. A stud that produces champions is much more valuable than an unproven stud.

Chapter VI
Pregnancy and Motherhood

INTRODUCTION

You are about to have puppies . . . or rather your dog is. The first rule is to RELAX; take some time to talk to your veterinarian about prenatal and whelping care, then sit back and wait 63 days from the day of breeding. Mark on your calendar the expected date—plus or minus a day or two—and prepare yourself. When the expected date rolls around, stay home. One friend of ours left the house in care of a babysitter and came home to find that the sitter had been midwife for 8 puppies—surely above and beyond the call of duty!

PREGNANCY

One of the problems of canine pregnancy is that we sometimes don't know if the dog is pregnant for several weeks after breeding. Rabbit tests for dogs do not exist. Some bitches, even though not pregnant, will exhibit symptoms of pregnancy, which can be misleading and disappointing, if you are hoping for a litter of pups. True pregnancy is unmistakable by around the fifth or sixth week, for the abdomen swells slightly, and the nipples become red and puffy. By the 35th day your veterinarian can eliminate any lingering doubts by a thorough examination. It is at this time he should give you dietary instructions, if any, and other relevant information.

Should your dog be pregnant, both you and the expectant mother will prepare. Nature provides for pregnant mothers by releasing hormones which increase maternal instincts, as well as the hormones which start labor and milk production. But since our dogs are a part

94

of us and we are responsible for their care, we can also help them through this period.

A pregnant bitch requires more food, but should not be overfed. Divide the meals into two, and supplement them with milk and biscuits in the middle of the day. Additional vitamins, A & D, may be advised and 2 to 4 teaspoons given daily is usually the rule depending on the size of the dog. Just before whelping time most dogs cut down on their food. There just isn't room for both the litter and meal. But see that she continues to eat something, especially light meals with meat and milk. You can encourage feeding by giving her favorite foods. In general, dogs thrive on high protein diets during pregnancy and if you have been feeding your dog her usual excellent diet, she should do well.

You must be sure she is exercised, *but* not too violently or under duress. All pregnant dogs should be kept from too much stair climbing and you should try to keep your dog from excited jumping up and down off beds and chairs, or roughhousing with children. One of the problems of pregnancy is constipation, and regular, sensible exercise as well as a good diet will help. You may have to use mineral oil as well to help alleviate this condition.

Your veterinarian will be able to tell within a month whether or not the bitch was successfully bred.

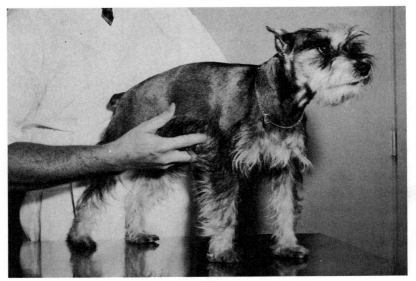

Keep the bitch's run sterilized throughout pregnancy. This will aid in preventing worm infestation.

Some doctors advocate worming around the third or fourth week. It would be best to check with your veterinarian, in any event, because he should prescribe the dosage or, even better, do the worming himself.

If your dog is unclipped, you can make it easier for the pups to nurse by trimming the hair around the nipples when she is almost ready to whelp. This helps prevent worm infestations and lost puppies.

In days past, before dog became man's best friend, a pregnant bitch, about to whelp, would make a nest. She might scratch a hole in the ground and root around until it was soft and comfortable. But nowadays dogs live in our houses or around them, and we are

Continue regular exercise during the first month of pregnancy.

responsible for a dog's "maternity room." A whelping box is easy to make and maintain. Some people give over the whole matter to the veterinarian and have the whelp at his hospital or a professional kennel with facilities. But most of us want to be near our dog when she whelps and may also want our families to watch. It is a wonderful way to introduce children to the marvels of motherhood, in a wholesome, natural way. You must, however, be sure that the spectators are instructed not to disturb the mother or pups during labor.

The whelping box is a low sided box which is roomy enough for the Miniature Schnauzer mother and her puppies. Your local pet supplier may be able to help you with your selection of a whelping box, but should a supplier be unavailable a homemade box can be constructed of wood with an additional one-inch ledge around the inside, in case your dog is an awkward mother with a tendency to sit on her offspring. One side should be hinged so that you may clean it easily.

When her time draws near, introduce the Miniature Schnauzer bitch to her whelping quarters.

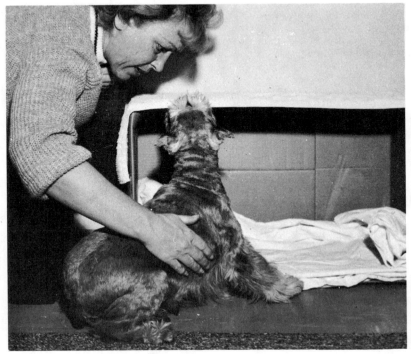

98

Once well along in pregnancy, it is quite all right to pamper the mother-to-be with extra attention.

Where do you put the whelping box? Probably the best place is the warm kitchen, but this may not be large enough or convenient for your family. Some dogs, especially Schnauzers, are happier in an out-of-way place. Any room which is warm and free from drafts will do. A cellar, unless it is very warm and dry, is not suitable. Besides the physical danger to mother and pups, you will spend your days going up and down stairs to attend to their needs. You want to be where you can see that all those wiggling balls of fur are not getting into trouble, in or out of the box.

Most dogs are used to their own beds or kennels. Be sure that you accustom your dog to her "maternity room," or you may find her whelping in a closet corner among the shoes or out in the garden under a bush.

But most of all, see that you have a peaceful home. You can forgive your dog an occasional upset stomach or indigestion. After all, there's no morning sickness or maternity clothes and the hospital bills are low. Maternity is a natural function of dogs and under happy, peaceful conditions, your dog can be expected to care for herself with little or no problem, requiring only a minimum of sympathetic assistance from you.

WHELPING

You have provided the whelping box, and the mother-to-be has been carefully fed and exercised, and examined by the veterinarian. Now you have your eye on the calendar. Perhaps you have an arrangement to bring your dog to the veterinarian when labor begins, or he is to come to the house. Your dog may start in the middle of the night, when you can't get help easily. Remember, if there is any trouble at all, call your veterinarian, regardless of the hour. A dog, whether she is a valuable show dog or a beloved family pet, deserves professional help if she cannot help herself.

Most dogs, however, bear their young easily. Certain breeds, because of selective breeding, may have had basic body changes, and whelping is difficult. Such difficulty is predictable and your veterinarian's advice will enable you to help the mother over the rough spots. Occasionally, a Caesarian is recommended. Reliable doctors will not suggest an operation unless it is an absolute necessity, because of danger to the mother and the problems of aftercare for the pups.

Be prepared should be our motto. Here is a list of things you can have ready when your dog is about to whelp: the whelping box, lined with newspaper, extra newspaper, towels, cotton, warm water, a scissors to cut the cord, thread to tie the cord, an electric heating pad or hotwater bottles, an eye dropper in case you have to feed the puppies, and if you happen to have them, a pair of scales to weigh the puppies as they are born. It is a good idea, especially if your puppies are pure-bred, to have a pad of paper and pencil to record markings, weight, time of arrival, etc., of each puppy.

How do you know when the event is about to begin? Your dog's behavior will tell you. She will start preparing a "nest," just as if you hadn't provided one for her. All those carefully arranged papers which you put in the whelping box will be torn up and arranged and rearranged. This is her first maternal act—making a home for her puppies. She will look distracted, restless, anxious, and start to pant. Probably, her last meal will be untouched or she may have some indigestion.

If you have taken her temperature before all these symptoms appear, it will be around normal, 101.5°. About 12 hours before labor begins, it drops radically to 97° or 98°. This is a sure sign. If it shoots up again, better call the doctor . . . something may be wrong!

If you must carry the pregnant bitch, carry her as demonstrated here by Lila Jones.

Real contractions are unmistakable. The dog will tense, hunch up, strain, relax. This is repeated over and over as she settles down to business. The contractions are widening the mouth of the womb and pushing the sac containing the first puppy towards the cervix, which is in the pelvis, now widening to receive this precious package. This is one reason for not allowing older dogs to breed for the first time. The bone and cartilage in the pelvic area harden as the dog grows older and cannot stretch during labor. If true contractions continue more than three or four hours without success, you had better call the veterinarian. This means that there is some problem with the bitch or foetus and delay may mean injury to your dog and the loss of the litter.

If your dog has trouble actually pushing her puppy out, you may be called upon as an assistant obstetrician. The most important things to remember are: *never* put your fingers into the dog's vagina,

Even during pregnancy, keep the Miniature Schnauzer clipped and well groomed.

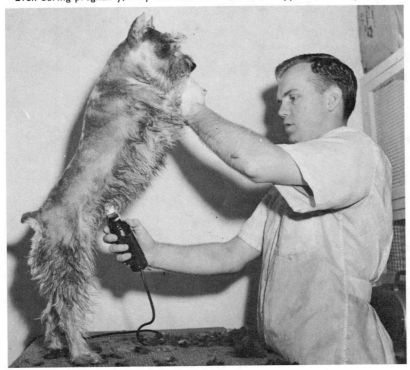

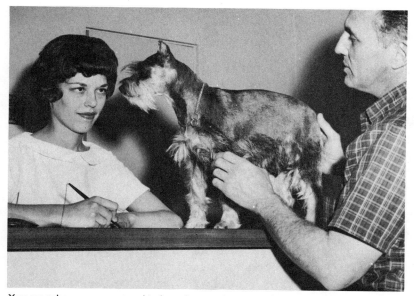

You can take your expectant bitch to the veterinarian to whelp under the professional care of a doctor.

and *never* force the puppy out, in any way. The best way you can aid your dog is, using a towel, hold onto the sac containing the puppy and gently apply traction to the puppy as it comes out with the contractions. This is only to prevent it from slipping back into the mother. Exert *no* pull at all. Once the puppy is out, a slight tug on the cord will help bring the placenta out too. If it looks as though your dog is having trouble whelping, call the veterinarian.

Whelping takes from 1 to 12 hours but an average litter of 4-5 puppies generally takes about 4 hours. Some take longer. And the puppies can arrive from 5 to 60 minutes apart. In between puppies, take your dog outside to relieve herself or even give her a little milk. But if she is not done whelping she will remain restless and continue straining.

Most puppies come into the world head first, although there are quite a number which make their debut feet first. Sometimes the puppy is preceded by a rush of water as the sac breaks, but more often it is born with the sac intact. The foetus develops in a sac filled with liquid. Each sac is attached to the mother by a band of flesh called the *placenta*. The umbilical cord connects the foetus and the placenta and nourishment from the mother is sent to the puppy through the cord. When the puppy is born, if the sac is still around it, the mother dog, her maternal instincts all working, will tear the sac off, cut the cord, and she will often eat the sac, cord, and placenta which follows it. Nowadays, it seems there are some lazy dogs, and their masters must help them whelp, or perhaps the puppies are arriving at such a rate that she has no time. If your dog cannot aid the puppy, or is too distracted with the next arrival, your help is essential. Break the sac and strip it back over the puppy. Cut the cord about 1-2″ from the navel and, if advised to do so by your veterinarian, tie the cord with a bit of silk string. Some doctors feel that the mother may worry over the string and nibble at it, causing infection. In most cases, there is little or no bleeding through the umbilical cord. The cord dries up and drops off in a few days.

When a puppy emerges, and the mother has stripped off the covering, she will lick and lick it and tumble it about until it is breathing normally, dry, moving and squealing. Sometimes she cannot do this, or the puppy may not start to breathe. Immediately take up the dog in a towel and massage it vigorously. Don't be

Four three-day-old Miniature Schnauzer puppies from the same litter. Note the difference in color.

The whelping box should permit the female easy entrance and exit.

afraid, you won't injure it. You may even hold it upside down and shake it to clear the lungs. If it still doesn't respond, artificial respiration is next. One method is to breathe into the dog's mouth until the lungs are filled and breathing starts. Or you can hold the dog with the navel away from you, grasp the cord with thumb and pinky and alternately pull the cord and press against his chest with the other three fingers. A third method is to raise and lower the legs rhythmically against the dog's chest. *Don't give up, your chances of success are good.* This often happens when the dog arrives feet first and the cord is pinched or cut before he is out; other pups may arrive this way, so you had better call the veterinarian if you need help.

With a Schnauzer and a large litter, you may want to provide a temporary nursery. A dog in hard labor may throw herself about and her helpless newborn pups can be crushed. Place a box near the mother so she can see her brood, and keep them warm with a hot water bottle wrapped in a towel or an electric heating pad. When you have checked that each little fellow is perking normally, put him in the box. If whelping takes long, and the puppies are crying, you can give them one or two dropperfulls of warm milk—one cup milk mixed with one teaspoon Karo is a good mixture.

But as soon as the mother is relaxed and labor is at an end, be sure to put the pups on her to nurse. The first milk of the mother, called *colostrum,* contains valuable vitamins and minerals and antibodies which give your puppy immunity to diseases while it is nursing. This first nursing also causes contractions in the uterus and helps expel any placental matter or even an unexpected puppy!

When the last puppy has arrived, your bitch is a new dog. She will be relaxed and easy. No more straining, no more anxiety. She will stretch out peacefully and count noses and then put her house to order. You can help by providing new papers and cleaning up.

It may seem impossible, with all that is going on, but you must try to keep count of the number of placentas which come out. There should be one for each puppy. Sometimes the placenta comes with the puppy, sometimes it follows with the next. But if placenta matter is left inside the dog, it can be very dangerous and your veterinarian should be called. Many dogs eat the placenta, cord and sac. When dogs were wild and not domesticated, this may have served as extra food, but today it is just as well if you remove this

About twelve hours before labor begins the bitch's temperature will drop to about 97°.

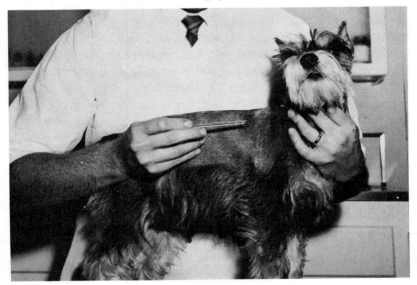

106

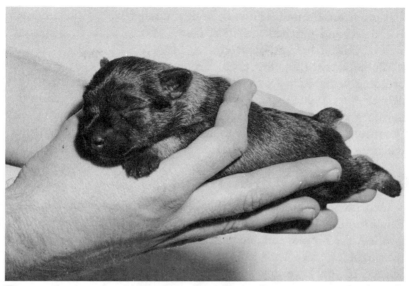

The eyes of a three-day-old puppy are closed. They will open on about the eleventh day.

material. You are interested in your dog's diet and won't let her starve, I'm sure!

Another thing breeders often advise is that you keep a record of the time of arrival of each puppy, his markings and weight, and any other characteristics.

Once in a great while a puppy is born with a deformity. This is very sad, and if the litter is small you will no doubt be quite upset. Harelip is one such congenital deformity, but today it is correctable by surgery. Oftentimes, with harelip, however, the puppy will also have a cleft palate. This prevents it from nursing properly and the dog will starve. Some puppies are born with other malformations, or perhaps the hind feet are turned as a result of the position in the uterus. Your veterinarian will tell you which of these conditions can be corrected and modern veterinary medicine has gone far in perfecting new surgical methods. Discuss your problems with your veterinarian and follow his instructions.

If you have no veterinarian in attendance be on the lookout for the following signs of trouble: labor lasting more than 4-6 hours with no success, excessive straining and pain, trembling and shivering with near exhaustion and collapse, vomiting. Puppies arriving feet first often mean more following in this manner with problems such as tangled and pinched umbilical cords. If any of these symptoms appear, call for help immediately.

We hope that these few problems have not discouraged you from breeding your bitch. Don't worry, most dogs have perfectly normal deliveries and your biggest problem will be to keep from taking the newborn pups away from their mother and cuddling them yourself. We mention problems mostly to help prepare you for any emergency which might arise when you have no professional help at hand.

FALSE PREGNANCY

Once in a great while, a bitch will show signs of pregnancy after being in heat, but will not be pregnant at all. Her abdomen will be swollen, the nipples red and puffy. These symptoms may disappear overnight or she may keep you in suspense until almost time to whelp. If you have any suspicions, consult your doctor. For one thing, if your dog was not impregnated, she may then be entitled to a return service, and your doctor should ascertain that there was no abortion or resorbing of the foetus. Also, false pregnancy is often a sign of illness or malfunctioning in the dog. Sometimes changes

Once all the puppies are born, offer the new mother some food and water.

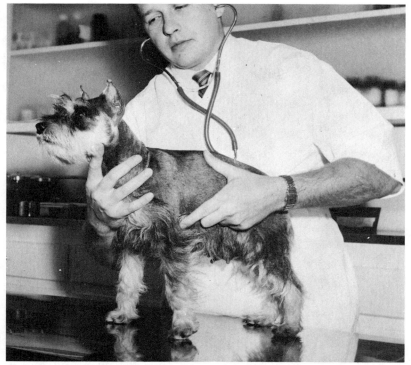

Should your bitch have difficulties while in whelp, immediately rush her to a veterinarian. Caesarean section has been successfully performed on Miniature Schnauzers, with both the mother and puppies coming through with flying colors.

are caused by tumors, cysts or infections. If you want your next breeding to be successful, you will have to be sure that your bitch is healthy.

AFTERCARE

The aftercare of your bitch is one of general good health routines. You may have to feed her more often, but be careful not to let her get too fat. Be sure that the diet is properly balanced with lots of protein and milk. If she seems a little constipated (after all, her insides have been severely jolted) a little mineral oil will help.

There is one thing to look out for in your nursing mother. Dogs which produce large amounts of milk or have very large litters often develop a form of convulsion known as *eclampsia* or suckling

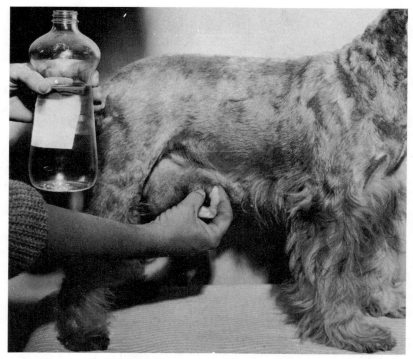

To prevent a Miniature Schnauzer's nipples from cracking soften them.

fits. This seems to be caused by a calcium deficiency caused by loss to the mother during nursing. If this happens, she will start to stagger, lose coordination and suffer from convulsions and often fall unconscious. Call your veterinarian immediately. The most common cure is large doses of calcium given by injection. Plenty of calcium after that can keep eclampsia from recurring.

Mastitis is another illness that can plague the dam. This is an infection of the breasts. It causes the milk to become extremely acid and this affects the puppies. It used to be thought that dam's milk had to be alkaline and that any acidity would be injurious to the puppies. This is untrue, as bitch's milk is either neutral or slightly acid naturally. Extreme acidity, however, like any extreme, is dangerous. Using limewater will not cure the condition. The mother dog must be seen by a veterinarian and medicated properly, as soon as possible. The puppies will have to be fed a substitute formula until she is cured, or else weaned altogether.

As for your newborn puppies, more in the next chapter, but there are one or two things to note. For the most part, puppies, like human babies, want to eat and sleep the first week. If they are unhappy about something, they cry.

If one of the puppies seems weaker than the others, put him on the rear nipples. These are bigger and he can get a better hold. You may even have to help him hang on if he has trouble. Another problem which occurs occasionally is when the mother fails to lick her puppy when he is newborn and stimulate elimination. This licking is the only way the puppy can be stimulated to urinate. If she doesn't do this, you are elected. But it's easy enough. Just rub the puppy's tummy and anus with a soft piece of cotton which is dampened with warm water and wait for the puddle. In a few days, he can manage it by himself and you will have plenty of puddles.

Chapter VII
Puppyhood

INTRODUCTION

Have you breathed a sigh of relief? Your dog has come through with flying colors; she has produced a lively, hungry, healthy litter of puppies. Not only that, she is taking care of them with all the love and vigilance a dog can command. Every single puppy is inspected each time it passes review in front of her; each is carefully washed and licked. And she provides her own built-in supply of milk, already bottled and warmed. When she leaves to eat or go outside for a breather, she rushes back afterwards and once again counts noses, just in case she lost one.

Indeed, the mother dog provides all that nature requires: food, warmth, cleanliness and love. When the puppies are old enough, she knows when to wean and how to wean them away from her.

Occasionally, however, problems arise and if so, your veterinarian can help you. Good medical advice and common sense care should prevent any mishaps.

THE NEST

In most cases, the whelping box also serves as the nursery until the puppies are old enough to sleep away from their mother. You may have to add to the sides as the puppies grow so they won't wander away. As long as you keep the papers changed and the box clean, there will be no problem. In addition, the doting mother helps keep the nest clean. She encourages the puppies to urinate and defecate and then cleans up the mess as well. After two or three

Puppies eat, sleep and play.

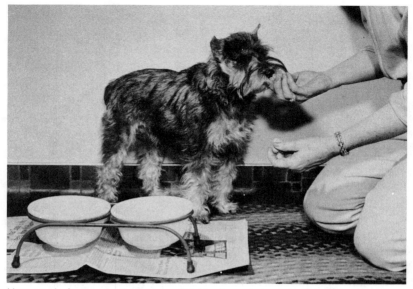

Have ample food and water at your bitch's disposal throughout lactation. Excellent easy-to-keep-clean utensils can be purchased at your pet shop.

weeks, however, she may stop, and then you become chambermaid. But take courage, it will soon be spring and then you can take the pups outdoors and your chores will become lighter.

Once in a while, if the mother is ill, or there are just too many demanding little fellows for her to handle, she may neglect to encourage elimination and cleanliness. If this occurs, you can help the puppies to urinate by rubbing their bottoms round and round just like the mother does with her tongue. If they are sore, rub a little vaseline in also. But you may have to clean up afterwards as well!!

If the mother, for some reason, is not in the nest to help warm the puppies, be sure to provide warmth. You can use an electric heating pad made just for this purpose. They are available at your petshop.

DIET

Most dams have an adequate supply of milk which lasts three to four weeks without supplementing. Occasionally, the litter may be so large or the milk so scanty that you have to help out. A foster mother is ideal, but available foster mothers (and willing owners) are hard to find. If you are so fortunate, you will find that it is not hard to accustom the new mother to her new pups. Rub a little of her milk on the puppies' tummies and let her lick it off. In no time at all, they are friends, and if you leave them in a quiet, out-of-the-way place, they will soon be old friends.

But suppose you are not so lucky, and you find that *you* are the substitute mother. It's back to baby bottles and formula for you! If your dog's milk is scanty, you may only have to supplement several times a day, but if you are a full-time puppy mother, plan on at least five or six feedings per day. Surprisingly, the care of a young puppy is very similar to that of a young baby, except that puppies grow up faster and you quit walking the floor sooner.

It is most convenient to make up a large amount of formula in advance, refrigerate it, and then pour it into bottles and warm it to body temperature for each feeding. Be sure that the holes in the nipple are large enough and that, while feeding, you are careful that the puppy does not take in too much air (tilt the bottle so that the top and nipple are always full).

There are several excellent brands of simulated bitch's milk on the market. Follow directions, refrigerate and that's all there is. You may want to ask your veterinarian which brand he recommends.

When puppies are two weeks old their eyes will be open.

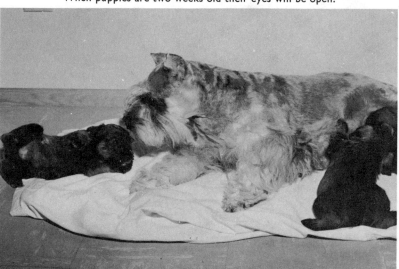

The ideal homemade formula? There are as many as there are veterinarians. If you are making your own, however, remember that cow's milk contains less fat (4%) than bitch's milk (11%). Here are three typical formulas you can try:

(1)	(2)	(3)
1 oz. cream	6 oz. evaporated milk	2 oz. lactogen
1 oz. Nestle's Pelargon	3 oz. water	2 oz. cream (30% butterfat)
6 oz. water	½ tbs. corn syrup	4 oz. water

Refrigerate and warm when needed.

How much do you feed a young puppy? Most dog owners say until his tummy is full and he just lolls back, almost too full to move. You can also tell when he is finished as a little milk will bubble around his mouth. But this doesn't tell you how much formula to prepare. The following chart should help, but remember, these are typical amounts and if your puppies are obviously hungry, feed them some more. If the one you select agrees with the pups, don't change. A change in the diet of a young puppy can be disastrous. This is a good point to remember if you are selling or giving puppies away when they have weaned. Give some of the same type of food

Check the weight of the puppy at regular intervals.

116

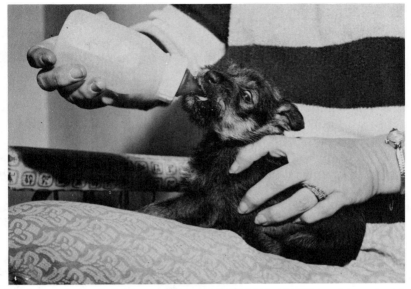

Puppies can be bottle-fed in an emergency. Artificial bitch's milk can be purchased at your pet shop.

you have been giving your puppies to the new owners, or include instructions, so that the puppy's diet does not change.

Amount of formula per feeding in ounces	Weight of puppy in pounds
1 oz.	¾ lb.
1¾ oz.	1 lb.
2 oz.	2 lbs.
2¾ oz.	3 lbs.

If you are only supplementing, you won't have to make up too much, but if you are feeding the puppies completely, better make up a two days' supply at once. Unless the puppies are very tiny, you can probably start them on dish feeding quite soon. If you are having trouble getting a young puppy to drink out of a dish (and after all, what has a dish to offer, it just isn't mother) try dipping its lips into the dish. Instinct will cause him to lick it up and before you know it, that smart fellow will have his mug in the dish and be lapping it up.

The above formulae can also be used when weaning the puppies until you put them on whole milk.

WEANING

Puppies will usually nurse for three to four weeks and then gradually slacken, but you can start weaning them yourself as early as 15 to 16 days, using the proper foods. If left to wean without your help, your mother dog will appear to be doing a most unladylike act—she will regurgitate partially digested food for her pups to eat. She isn't sick; this is just instinctive with dogs. Wild dogs, having no prepared puppy meal or canned and packaged foods, used this as the first food for their helpless puppies, but you can start the puppies on supplementary foods and relieve your dog of this chore. By now your puppies are much livelier and their eyes are open. They are aware of the world—their mother and their box and those strange people who make cooing noises at them. They may even have tried a little exploring and fallen out of the box once or twice. They wobble a bit, it is true, but they are on their feet, almost.

All this activity and the activity to come mean that the foods you give your dogs now are important. There are excellent preparations on the market for your newly weaned puppy. Use any of the puppy

The mother's milk provides the puppies with temporary immunity against several diseases.

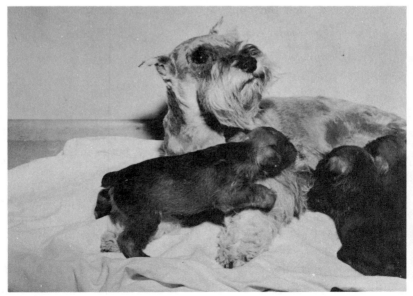

meals; they contain all the necessary nutrients for a rapidly growing pup. Many breeders feel that Pablum or baby cereals are not nutritious enough for such explosive growth, but people do use them with no apparent ill effects. If you use puppy meal or any cereal food, be sure to add milk and fat.

One way of getting a puppy to take to his new diet is to put a little on your finger and let him lick it off. Before you know it, he'll be licking the platter clean. Some people also add scraped beef to a puppy's diet. This is a bother to make, but you may feel it is necessary.

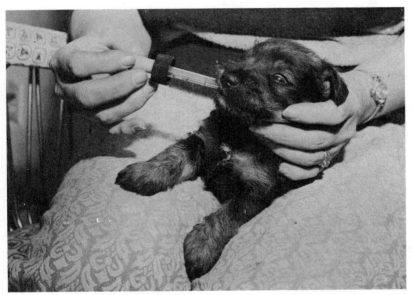

A puppy can be given medicine with an eyedropper.

Using a spoon or the back of a knife, scrape along the piece of beef (bottom round is fine) so that what you get is almost liquid beef, beef minus the gristle and connective tissue. Vitamins and mineral supplements are also recommended.

We like to see each puppy with his own dish. This is because the runts (there are often some in the litter) sometimes get pushed aside by the bigger pups; this method gives every puppy his share. Be sure also to have a water dish with fresh water available.

When the puppy is two to four days old, the tail can be docked. Photo by Al Barry of Three Lions, Inc.

Here is a typical feeding schedule for your weaned puppy.

Age	7 a.m.	Noon	5 p.m.	10 p.m.
4 to 12 weeks	x	x	x	x
3 to 6 months	x	x	x	
6 to 12 months	x		x	
1 year and on			x	

Gradually increase the amount of food you give the dog if he needs it. An active dog requires more food than a dog that is penned up most of the time.

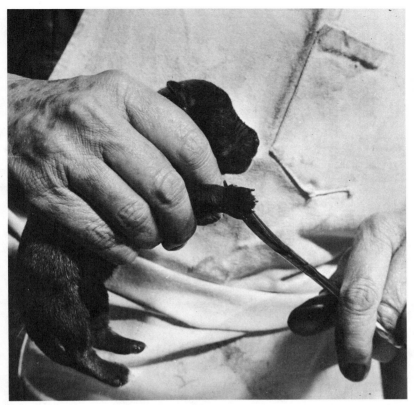

Dewclaws can be removed at tail-cropping time. Photo by Al Barry of Three Lions, Inc.

DEWCLAWS

Dewclaws are small vestigial claws found on the lower legs of some breeds. If your dog is born with dewclaws it is best to trim them off. Because the nails are not worn down as are the other nails on a dog's feet, they can become ingrown and cause infection. Dewclaws can be cut off by the third or fourth day.

WORMING

Chapter XII describes parasites and how they infect dogs. You may be surprised to learn, however, that very young puppies can be infested with parasites, which they pick up from their mother's body, possibly even before they are born. Three-week-old puppies

121

You can let a buyer select a puppy when it's two weeks old, but don't sell it until it is at least seven weeks of age.

can be wormed with no harmful results. Some breeders worm their litters as a matter of course and don't wait until the parasites put in an appearance. By then it is often too late. Consult with your veterinarian about dosages or let him do it if you are nervous. When worming is done, be sure that your puppies are in good health, or any dose, no matter how safe it is ordinarily, will be harmful. Follow the veterinarian's advice exactly.

TEETH

Puppies, like human babies, are not born with teeth, although there are always exceptions. And like humans, they have two sets of teeth, first or baby teeth and second teeth. The first baby teeth to erupt are the incisors (front teeth). These push out by about 4-5 weeks, and after them come the canines (these are like our eye teeth). The incisors fall out at about 4-5 months and the canines a month or so later. The molars arrive at 5 months, 6 and 7 months. A dog has a full complement of 42 teeth, 20 in the lower jaw and 22 in the upper.

When the teeth are erupting, if the puppy has any illness the enamel will not be deposited on the teeth or the teeth may be pitted or discolored. If the first teeth have not fallen out and the second are arriving, you may have to have the first teeth pulled so that the others will come in straight.

Veterinarians advise that you have your dog's teeth cleaned regularly, as tartar often coats them heavily and then it is difficult to remove.

HERNIA

As your puppy grows, you may see a small lump over the navel. This means that the navel has failed to heal properly and the bulge is a hernia. If the deformity is slight, there is no danger, but if the opening in the abdomen is large enough, a loop of intestine can work

A cardboard ruff can be made to prevent your puppy from scratching his cropped ears. Photo by Al Barry of Three Lions, Inc.

out into the sac. You will have to have your veterinarian repair the hernia or strangulation might occur.

SPECIAL CHARACTERISTICS OF THE MINIATURE SCHNAUZER PUPPY

Two grooming aids are performed on Miniature Schnauzer puppies. The tail must be docked and the ears are usually cropped, except in states which forbid cropping.

DOCKING THE TAIL

In most cases the tail is docked on the fourth day. This does not appear to bother the puppies at all. Your veterinarian should do it, but if you should have to do it yourself, it is not too difficult. Using a sterile scissors (boil first), you first pull the skin of the tail back and cut the tail at the first or second joint. Then pull the skin forward, and it will form a flap that heals over the cut.

CROPPING EARS

Many Miniature Schnauzers have their ears cropped, although there are some states where this is illegal. In states where it is not

Some states do not permit a dog's ears to be cropped.

Place the ruff around the puppy's neck and fasten it into position. Photo by Al Barry of Three Lions, Inc.

The puppy will appear sad for a while, but his future handsome appearance makes it all worth while. Photo by Al Barry of Three Lions, Inc.

When you buy your Miniature Schnauzer puppy, have a dog bed waiting for him. Your pet shop has a wide selection.

allowed, the AKC regulations do not require cropped ears for Miniature Schnauzers. The ears are cropped by the eighth week. It must be done by a veterinarian, who will put the dog under anesthesia so that the cropping is painless. The ear is cut from the rounded base to the top of the flap of the ear, where it is trimmed to a fine point. The ears are protected, often by tape, until healed.

A MINIATURE SCHNAUZER PUPPY DIET

Miniature Schnauzers are small but active dogs. They need, as do other puppies, bone-building foods, meat, milk and fat. The following amounts of food are recommended for your Miniature Schnauzer. Of course, if the pup wants more or less, make any changes necessary. No dog should be forced to eat more than he wants or allowed to go very hungry.

Age	7 a.m.	Noon	5 p.m.	10 p.m.
Weaning to 3 months	½ cup Pablum or puppy meal, with warm water or milk	½ cup warm milk with cereal	2 tbs. chopped beef, 2 tbs. cereal or meal, vitamin supplement	½ cup warm milk mixed with puppy meal or Pablum

Age	7 a.m.	Noon	5 p.m.	10 p.m.
3 to 6 months	½ cup meat with shredded wheat or cereal or puppy meal	1 cup milk, soft boiled eggs (twice a week) or 1 cup cottage cheese	½ cup meat with ½ cup dog meal or kibble and water	
6 to 12 months	½ cup dog meal or cereal with cottage cheese or egg, plus milk		½ cup meat with ¾ cup kibble or meal, fat, scraps	

Be sure to add fat for a healthy coat and skin. Also, you can gradually change from Pablum or puppy meal to dog meal or kibble as the puppy grows older.

PHYSICAL CHARACTERISTICS

A three-month Miniature Schnauzer looks like his mother or father except that his proportions are different. His head and paws

A collar and lead will help in keeping your puppy safe from cars, and also aid in training him. Plain and fancy collars and leads can be purchased at your local pet shop.

See your pet shop for the latest canine fashions.

This metal dog bed is just the right size for a Miniature Schnauzer.

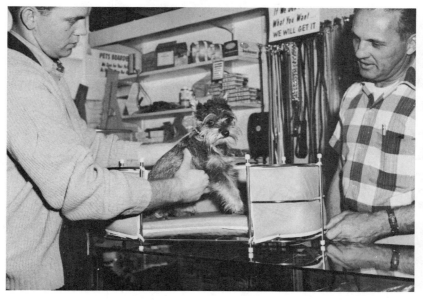

While at the pet store, get your puppy a safe toy.

Selection can be difficult. One Miniature Schnauzer is as cute as the other.

Your pet shop has a wide selection of safe dog toys.

Never pick up a young Miniature Schnauzer by his front legs.

This four-month-old Miniature Schnauzer appreciates love and attention.

Never give your Miniature Schnauzer candy meant for humans. Buy him dog treats instead.

appear large and awkward. But these differences fade as he grows older. Your puppy should be square in general outline, well built and sinewy. The forelegs should be straight, shoulder sloping and neck arched. The coat should be hard and wiry, although some of the puppy fur is still visible. Many puppies are trimmed by nine weeks, especially on the head. The tail is short and carried well. Puppies may be awkward, but their walk should be brisk, with one foot in front of the other, not crossed over.

REGISTRATION PAPERS FOR PUREBRED DOGS

There are two steps in registering a purebred dog with the American Kennel Club. First the owner of the litter must send in a litter application with all the details properly filled in. This is sent to the American Kennel Club, 51 Madison Avenue, New York, New York 10010. When the dog is purchased, the new owner can apply for an individual certificate, with the dog's name and pedigree. If a certificate already exists, all the new owner must do is have the registration papers transferred to his name.

And, of course, your town may require a dog license, which has nothing to do with pedigree. Be sure and check on the town's regulations for vaccinations, if any, and unleashed dogs.

COMMON DISEASES OF PUPPYHOOD

In Chapter XII diseases are discussed in detail, so this section includes only a few of the common diseases.

Infected Navel: In a small puppy watch out for an infected navel. This is often caused by rough or hard surfaces in the nest. The navel is rubbed and becomes infected. The veterinarian will have to clean it and medicate. The best prevention is to provide a soft bed for your puppies.

Five-week-old Miniature Schnauzers can be kept bright-eyed with proper food and care.

Distemper: Distemper is a disease which infects many puppies. It is often fatal or it leaves the puppy with nervous ailments or other serious after effects. Until a puppy is weaned, he is safe, but after that, you must protect him with vaccine. If your puppy becomes feverish, his nose and eyes runny, and his stomach upset, consult your veterinarian immediately. The health of the whole litter is at stake.

Hard Pad: This ailment is most infectious to young puppies. They run a high fever with intestinal upsets. The foot pads are very tender. Call your veterinarian for treatment.

Parasites: We have already mentioned worming, but you can still keep an eye out for parasites such as fleas and ticks. They can infect a puppy at any age. If you keep the nest and other sleeping areas clean, there is less danger.

Deficiency Diseases: To prevent problems such as rickets or other deficiency diseases, be sure that your puppy's food is nourishing and well balanced. Remember that he is growing rapidly and needs more protein in the form of milk and meat, and more fat and vitamins than his elders.

Photograph illustrates the difference between cropped and uncropped ears.

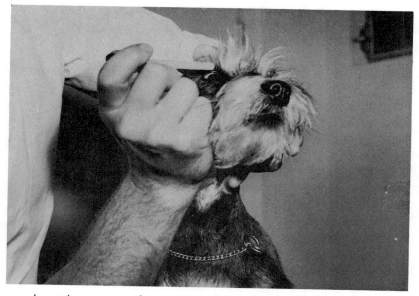
Leave the treatment of eyes to the professional hands of the veterinarian.

Eye Infections: Once in a while, a tiny puppy's eyes become infected even before they open. The corner of the eye can be lifted up, the eye drained and medicated. See your veterinarian.

Diarrhea: When a puppy has diarrhea it is viewed as a serious condition. It may be caused by a change in the diet, spoiled food, or may be a symptom of a more serious illness. Your veterinarian should be contacted at once.

Chapter VIII
Diet

A TYPICAL MINIATURE SCHNAUZER DIET

Miniature Schnauzers of one year of age or over may be small, but they are very active. Just following you around the house uses up a lot of energy . . . to say nothing of chasing the local cats and barking at menacing strangers. They need plenty of food to supply all this energy. Feed your dog twice a day if necessary. For a normal size Miniature Schnauzer, plan on an evening meal consisting of ¾ cup of meat, ¾ cup of dog food, and fat. You can use water to mositen, or perhaps milk. Your dog will also welcome an occasional coddled egg, or cottage cheese. If you also give your Miniature a morning meal, give him half the evening meal or several dog biscuits.

THE MINIATURE SCHNAUZER DIET IN GENERAL

Are you being watched by soulful eyes? Is every bite you eat at dinner followed by your dog, standing there licking his chops, as you put away a steak? And do you give in and slip him just a little bit, or a bone to gnaw on? DON'T, if you want your dog to be healthy as well as polite.

A well-fed, well-trained dog eats, at *his* dinner hour, only what you put in *his* dish. Encouraging dogs to eat food at other times only makes them dinner pests. It may also harm them nutritionally. Bad habits at the dinner table can lead a dog to beg from other people and this is even more dangerous. You know what's in your dinner plate, but unless the ladies have been exchanging recipes over the back fence, you may not know what your neighbor is feeding your dog.

There is, of course, the possibility that you have not been feeding your dog properly and that he is genuinely hungry. Whether he is hungry or just badly trained is for you to discover, but if it is malnutrition, symptoms will appear sooner or later. Surely it is wiser to check your pet's diet and see that it is made up of the essentials every dog needs.

When dogs were not yet domesticated, they ate what they killed, muscle, meat, innards, skin, bones, even the fur or hair. But we don't allow our dogs to forage for their own food any more (nor is there wild game available except in distant wooded areas) and we are responsible for giving them a proper meal. We must replace the ingredients which nature intended them to eat and which were found in the wild game they ate.

THE ELEMENTS OF A GOOD DIET

The essentials of your dog's diet are protein, carbohydrate, fats, vitamins and minerals. Each of these elements should be included in your dog's diet if he is to grow properly, look and feel healthy. Lack of any of the five essentials can cause a number of diseases, most of which are discussed in Chapter XII. Too much of any diet essential can also be harmful, however. People who feed their dogs all the best foods and then give them an extra dose of vitamins or minerals "just for good measure" may cause a toxic reaction in their pets. *Everything good in moderation* is a good motto for a proper diet.

PROTEINS

Proteins are found in meat, fish, some vegetables (such as soy bean) milk and cheese. They are used for essential body building. Meat can be fed your pet if it is fresh, dried or frozen (and thawed). If meat is dried, be sure that it is labeled "Vacuum Packed" as this process preserves the vitamins. Twenty to thirty percent of your dog's meal should be protein. If your dog is pregnant or nursing, she will need extra protein, and so do rapidly growing puppies.

CARBOHYDRATES

Carbohydrates should make up between 50 and 70% of your pet's dinner. They are found in cereals, vegetables, sugar, syrup and

A well-fed Miniature Schnauzer will always appear alert and healthy. Feed a commercial dog food for a well-balanced diet.

honey. Carbohydrates give a dog his boundless energy and help him grow. When starches are baked, the starches are converted into dextrin which tastes sweet. Most dogs have a sweet tooth and enjoy something sweet and tasty. But if you feed your dog too much carbohydrate, his diet will suffer, as he will eat less protein.

FATS

Fats are also important in a dog's daily ration. Bitch's milk naturally has more fat content than cow's milk, but once a dog is on adult food, he can drink regular milk, and not the enriched formula you fed him as a puppy. You must then add fat to his meal in other ways. This element is important as a vitamin reserve and as an aid for digestion by slowing the passage of food through the animal's intestine. It also keeps his coat healthy and shiny. Fat provides $2\frac{1}{4}$ times as much energy as an equivalent amount of carbohydrate or protein, but you cannot give a dog too much fat, as this may cause diarrhea. Naturally a dog which uses up a tremendous amount of energy, such as a hunting dog, can use more, but for most family dogs too much fat will lead to trouble. Your dog's diet should have about 5% fat content (and not more than 25%) to be nourishing. Important sources of fats are butter, suet, lard, bacon fat and even vegetable shortening. An excellent and cheap fat is bacon fat or grease from your cooking. Fatty meat is far better than lean cuts, so do not think you are being kind if you buy only the best quality top round steak for your dog; he'll probably look underfed and his coat and skin will suffer.

VITAMINS

Vitamins are those elusive substances without which we would all be undernourished and diseased. They were first discovered by Casimir Funk, a Polish scientist, in 1911. You must see that your dog has a certain amount of vitamins, but remember that if you are feeding your dog a good diet, he will probably get all the vitamins he needs. Pregnant and nursing mothers and pups need supplements, however.

MINERALS

Minerals are also found in many foods and need not be supplemented unless there is a specific need for more. Minerals such as calcium and phosphorus are used to build bones and teeth and are found in milk, vegetables, eggs, soy beans, bone marrow, blood, liver and some cereals (whole grained).

Following is a table of vitamins and minerals, their use in the body and where they are found.

See your pet shop for safe and easy to keep clean water utensils.

VITAMINS

A (and carotene)	*Use*	*Found in*
Stable at boiling temperatures	General living and growth	Alfalfa-leaf meal
Spoiled if exposed to air	Skin health	Butter, carrots
Stored in body	Fertility, Hearing,	Egg yolks, carotene
Fat soluble	Digestion, Vision,	Fish liver, oil
	Nerve health,	Glandular organs
	Prevention of infection	Leaves of plants
	Muscle coordination	Many dark green
	Pituitary gland function	vegetables

B Complex

Biotin, Pantothenic Acid	Growth, Appetite, Fertility, Nerve and Heart	Yeast, cereals
Riboflavin, Thiamine	health, Liver and gastro-	Eggs, milk, liver,
Folic Acid, Niacin	intestinal function	alfalfa meal
Pyrodoxin		Rapidly growing
Water soluble, some destroyed by high heat	Lactation, Intestinal absorption	plants
		Bacterial growth
Biotin negated by raw egg whites	Muscle function, Blood health, Bladder and kidney function	Cattle paunch and intestinal contents
	Prevention of anemia, black tongue and Vincent's disease	

D

Irradiated ergosterol	Regulates calcium and phosphorus in blood	Fish liver and oil
Stored by body and can stand heat		Some animal fats
Resists decomposition	Regulates Metabolism	
Fat soluble	Normal skeletal development and muscular coordination	
	Lactation	
	Prevents rickets	

E

Tocopherol	Survival of young puppies	Seed germ and
Stored in body		germ oils
Spoils if exposed to air		
Stand ordinary cooking temperatures		
Fat Soluble		
Unsaturated fatty acids	Coat and skin health	Wheat germ oil
		Linseed oil
		Other seed oils

K

Fat soluble	Blood clotting	Alfalfa-leaf meal
Antidote for Warfarin rat poison		

MINERALS:

Calcium		
90% stored in bones	Bones, teeth, blood component	Bones and bone meal
	Lactation, Fertility	Milk
	Muscle, nerve, heart function	Alfalfa-leaf meal
Phosphorus		
Stored in bones, blood, muscles and teeth	Bones, teeth	Cereals, milk
	Carbohydrate and Fat metabolism	Fish, bones, meat (generally abundant in dogs diet)
	Blood component	
	Liquid content of tissues	
Iron		
Need in minute amounts	Red blood cells	Egg yolk, liver
Stored in body—65% in blood; 30% in liver, marrow, spleen; 5% in muscle tissue	Transports oxygen in blood	Innards, bone marrow
	Prevents anemia	Meat
Potassium		
	Body fluid regulator	Blood
	Blood regulator	Vegetables, potatoes
	Muscle function	
Sodium		
Found in body with phosphorus, chlorine and sulphur	Regulates body fluids, blood	Table salt
	Component of gastric juices and urine	Blood
Chlorine		
	Same as above	
Iodine		
Found in thyroid gland	Thyroid health, metabolism	Foods grown in iodine-rich soil
		Fish meal from salt water fish
Magnesium		
Needed in tiny amounts	Muscles, bones	Bones, vegetables
	Nerve and blood function	
	Growth	
Copper		
Needed in tiny amounts	Forms hemoglobin with iron	Blood, copper sulphate
Sulphur		
Needed in tiny but regular amounts	Body regulation	Meat, egg yolks

CALORIES

Calories are not ingredients of food, but the unit used to measure heat—and food when it is eaten, digested and used can be measured in terms of calories. We are all of us very conscious of weight nowadays. We must not only watch our own figures but our dog's as well.

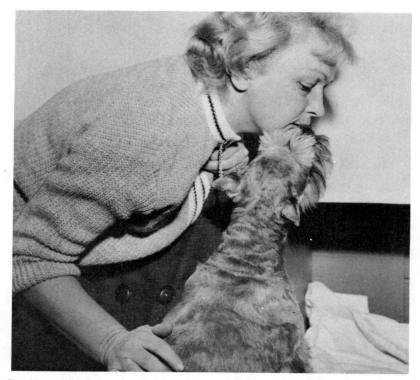

Should your Schnauzer have bad breath from some upsetting food, you can purchase a special canine breath sweetener at your pet shop.

Dogs can eat 30 to 50 percent more food than they need and still be hungry. Very small dogs, between 5 and 10 pounds, need 250 to 600 calories daily. Dogs weighing between 15 and 25 pounds use at least 600 to 1,000 calories and dogs from 30 to 60 pounds use up 1,100 to 2,000 calories. If your dog is eating more than he should, you may have to put him on a diet, or hope for a dog-type food substitute. Check the caloric value of the food you serve your dog.

COMMON TYPES OF DIETS

You now know the elements of a proper diet for your dog, but you may be wondering how to apply all this knowledge to what to put into your dog's dinner plate. There are a number of different types of diets available. Your pocketbook and the type of household you have will determine what kind of food you feed your dog. Your dog's size will dictate how much food you must provide. Certain types of hounds are deliberately kept thin, but most dogs look and feel best when their bodies are filled out, their coats glossy and the skin healthy. This is achieved with a proper diet. Remember that puppies will eat much more than adult dogs in terms of their weight, and that active dogs will consume more than their less active canine brothers.

CANNED DOG FOOD

Canned dog food is very cheap and very easy to prepare—a can opener is all you need. But be sure if you use this as the staple diet of your dog, that you know the true cost of the food and the protein content. Most canned dog food contains 70-75% water and the remaining 25% is food. A good-sized dog will need at least one can

Pet shops carry a variety of sanitary feeding dishes.

Scientifically prepared foods fed to these Miniature Schnauzers have kept them in excellent health.

of dog food a day, if it is not supplemented with other foods, regardless of what the label tells you. Another thing to watch out for is the quality of the canned food, although this may be difficult to discover. It is sad, but true, that many canned dog foods are not high quality and that the meat is of such low quality that you would never knowingly feed it to your pet. There are some good quality products, of course, put up by companies genuinely concerned with your dog's health and well being. Compare the protein and fat guarantees printed on the label. The more of each, the better the food. Or ask your veterinarian to recommend a good canned dog food and check the label for content. The Dept. of Agriculture issues a seal of approval for canned dog food which meets minimum nutritional standards.

KIBBLES WITH MEAT AND VEGETABLES

Kibbles are a form of biscuit but they are by no means a complete diet. Flour is the chief ingredient and as it is baked it is converted into dextrin which tastes sugary. Dogs love it and lick their lips for more. But the baking process destroys the vitamin and mineral content while it increases its dog appeal. Therefore you must add meat, vegetables and, often, vitamin and mineral supplements. You may find it is a nuisance to mix. If kibbles are used with no other added foods, this menu can cause serious diet deficiency diseases and even convulsions.

PELLETS

A number of commercial dried dog foods are available in pellet form. They can be eaten dry or with a little water, and extra water served on the side. Their chief attraction seems to be that they are easy to pour and "look nice."

MEALS (OR DRY DOG FOOD)

By far the most popular food in kennels is dog meal. It is also the most versatile of the packaged dog foods. All the essential vitamins and minerals are added in sufficient quantities, as well as protein. Some brands carry as much as 30% protein. If you use 1½ ounces of fat to 5 ounces of high quality meal, you have a dinner that cannot be surpassed for quality, nourishment and dog satisfaction. As an added

If fed properly, your Miniature Schnauzer can meet the demands of the most strenuous training.

inducement, it is easy to prepare, and extremely economical. Pregnant and nursing mothers will need extra milk and meat with their regular dinner. Special puppy meals are also available for growing dogs.

EXTRUDED FOODS

Extruded foods are a fairly new product made in the same way as puffed wheat or rice. The granules of starch are heated under great pressure and when the pressure is suddenly released, the granules explode—they are shot from guns as the ads say! Of course, this food tastes sweet and is enthusiastically greeted by dogs and you may think that this is an ideal food. But this eagerness may be hunger— real hunger. The food is blown up to twice its original size, and therefore the animal eats only one half his usual ration and he is full. But he is only getting one half his needs. The results are hunger and undernourishment, surely a poor investment for your pet.

DIET COST

Following is a table showing the various diets and their relative cost, based on feeding a 25-pound dog 900 calories a day. The prices may vary somewhat, depending on where you live.

	Type of Diet	Cost per day	Cost per year
1.	Table scraps	$ .50	$182.50
2.	Canned dog food (2 for 29c.)	.29	105.85
3.	Kibbles, meat, vegetables, supplement vitamins—18c. per lb., others app. vitamin supp. 5c. per day)	.38	138.70
4.	Pellets 15c. per pound	.084	30.66
5.	Dry dog food plus fat (14c. per pound for meal, fat free from your table)	.04	14.60

The above list shows that the last type of diet is by far the most economical. The authors suggest that when you are planning your first trip to the market or pet store for supplies for your new pet, that you take this book along or a list of the necessary elements for a good diet. Check the contents of each type of dog food and the cost.

Once you find a good nutritious diet for your dog, stick to it, as changes can cause intestinal upsets, especially in puppies. Of course, if your dog is hardy and has a good digestion, you may find yourself adding leftovers to his basic diet, especially those he loves. But be

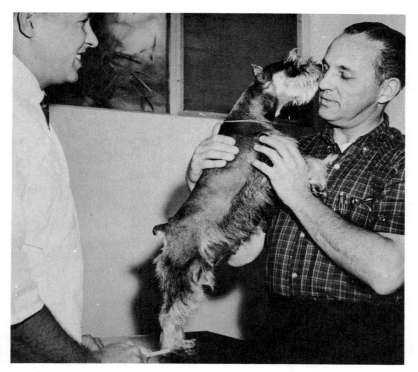

Lactating bitches require extra food, plus vitamins and minerals.

sure that these tidbits do not take the place of the really important proteins, vitamins and minerals. For a treat, you can give your dog biscuits or dog yummies. A friend with a large, active, almost grown dog finds that biscuits are a fine substitute for furniture. Whenever she finds that her dog is about to test the durability of the sofa, she gives him a handful of dog treats and this satisfies him.

QUANTITY

Just how much do you give a dog? Breeders recommend that you plan on $\frac{1}{2}$ to 1 ounce of food per pound of body weight, depending on the amount of exercise and the age of the dog. Feed your dog once or, in winter, twice a day. Oftentimes, in winter, dogs appreciate a light breakfast in order to help them face the school bus, mailman, garbage man and other sundry daytime activities. The main meal, however, should be given in late afternoon or early evening.

WATER

Have water available at all times. If you do not wish to keep the water dish out, offer water at least three times a day. You may want to restrict water to a puppy just before night, or in the case of illness.

DISHES

The best type of dishes are aluminum, but you can also purchase plastic or ceramic feeding pans. They do not chip or break easily, and can be cleaned quickly. Be sure that feeding and water pans are clean at all times. When you set out your dog's dinner, allow him at least 20-30 minutes to eat it, but then take it away and do not feed your dog until his next regularly scheduled meal time. This keeps him from being finicky and picky about his food. Naturally, if he is ill or has some diet problems, you will have to adjust. Another hint is to be sure that the food is not too sloppy and watery, so it's not messy.

Put your dog's dish in the same place at every feeding, preferably a spot where he won't be disturbed.

SPECIAL FEEDING PROBLEMS

Pregnant Bitches: Pregnant bitches need extra food, especially meat and milk, as well as extra vitamins. Feed your dog as much as she wants, but make sure that she doesn't get overweight. Toward the end of her pregnancy, keep the meals light.

Nursing mothers: Lactating bitches also need extra food, with meat, milk and vitamins especially essential. You may find it better to give her several meals a day so her milk will be rich.

Weaning: The chapter on puppyhood (Chapter VII) discusses puppy diet. The main thing to remember is that bitch's milk is richer than cow's milk and that when the puppies are weaned, you will have to add fat to the milk you feed them. You must also plan that puppies eat much more than adult dogs of the same size. Once they grow up their food intake will stabilize, but while they are growing, be sure to feed them highly nutritious foods and rich milk. There are several excellent puppy foods which can be mixed with milk and used for puppies.

Reducing: Overweight is a national concern. Everyone is on a diet, it seems, and diet foods and fads are a billion dollar business in this country. Your dog may not be conscious of his or her figure, but you should be aware of it. Fat dogs are prone to illness and unfit for showing. But dieting is heartrending. After all your dog doesn't know what it is all about and he can't rejoice in every lost pound on the scale. You MUST resist his appeals for more food, and tell your children (sternly) not to feed him, also.

To help a dog reduce, cut his caloric intake down so that he must live on his stored fat. If your dog normally eats 900 calories, then cut him down to 500. One cup of dog meal plus water should be enough. In ten days he will have lost about 1 pound. Exercise is also helpful. Check with your veterinarian for a proper diet for your pet if he is overweight.

Chapter IX
Training

PRINCIPLES OF TRAINING YOUR MINIATURE SCHNAUZER

In today's world of fast-moving cars and crowded cities and suburbs, the life of a dog is truly a *dog's life* if he is improperly trained. The many hazards of living mean the survival of the fittest—and to be fit for today's world a dog must be properly trained to obey his master (or mistress).

The methods are standard with dog trainers—positive training which relies on encouragement and reward, either by praise from the trainer or food, and negative training where mistakes are punished. Combinations of these methods are common.

With either reward or punishment, animal training requires that each step be taught slowly and completely before the next step is introduced. Rewards (positive training) can be *praise* by tone of voice and petting, or *food* such as a favorite tidbit, dog candy or biscuits. Dogs trained negatively with punishment—and some trainers advocate switches or chains thrown near the dogs, paper, or hitting—may become vicious. By and large, most dogs respond to violence in kind. Dogs are not born vicious; they are made so. The uncontrollable dog could have been saved by thoughtful training work when he was young or less wild. Sadly, in most cases, the dog who is mean or wild has to be destroyed, or is killed as a result of his foolhardy actions.

There are two types of training your dog can have—*general training* which makes it possible for him to live with the family in peace, and *specialized training* to qualify for the AKC Obedience

At first the puppy may balk when taught to walk on a lead, but it won't take long and he'll be walking proudly at your side.

Trials. Of course, you can also teach your dogs many tricks such as playing dead or begging, for your own enjoyment. Hunting dogs, police and army dogs, and other working breeds need special training. It is most often taught by experts in the field rather than by lay persons.

When you begin training remember the following: your puppy is anxious to obey you, and is really trying hard even if he doesn't quite succeed at first. Every ounce of puppy love wants to please you. If he can't quite make it the first time, be PATIENT. He will make the grade in time when his muscles are all working properly and he has mastered the first steps. Be CONSISTENT. Use the same word for the same command, and react the same way to his success or lack of success. Don't laugh at something he does one time and then punish him for it the next. Use your VOICE, not your hand, to punish. Very little can be accomplished by beating a dog except to frighten him.

Teach your dog ONE STEP AT A TIME. He can't learn the more complicated actions until he has mastered the elementary ones. REWARD your dog immediately if he does it right. Although you can use a treat, we believe that by complimenting your dog and showing him with your voice and mannerisms what a wonderful dog he is, how marvelously well he has learned to sit and how pleased everyone is with him, that he will answer with just oodles of love and willingness to learn more. PUNISH your dog if he refuses or disregards your commands by speaking angrily to him and making him realize that you are displeased; do not use violence or withhold basic necessities such as food.

The authors believe that the best and most enduring type of training is positive training, using only the master's voice in praise. Dogs trained with candy or other foods come to rely on this rather than on the person making the command. Of course, this does not mean that you should not occasionally reward your obedient dog with a bit of his favorite food. In extreme cases, you may have to use punitive measures once in a while to convince him of the error of his ways, but this should not be the standard training method for your dog.

HOUSEBREAKING

Do you have a new puppy? Or has one of the litter remained behind? The very first training you will have to start is *housebreaking*.

Teach your dog not to come begging for food at your table.

This is imperative if everyone is to live together harmoniously and in clean quarters. But puppies, like children, cannot be completely trained until they are more mature physically. When you hear of a toilet trained child of nine months, you can be sure that his mother is trained, not the baby. And so it is with dogs. Most dogs cannot be completely and reliably housebroken until four months of age, when their bladder and anus are under control. This is no cause for despair, however; there is plenty you can do until then to keep the house and your dog's quarters clean.

Most dogs are first paper-broken, unless they live outdoors. A dog will not deliberately mess his bed, but he will look around for a convenient corner. The first thing you must do with a young puppy is to confine him to a fairly small space and cover that space with newspaper. Then he can mess to his heart's content.

If you allow your puppy freedom of the house, you are asking for trouble. But if he does get out and make a puddle right in the middle of the floor, be sure to wipe it up thoroughly. Use a special dog scent to remove the odor, or your dog will make a beeline for that spot the minute he escapes again. Once he is trained, you can gradually allow him the run of the house, but keep an eye on him for danger signs.

Dogs instinctively use the same place over and over again. Observe which corner he calls his own, and gradually begin removing the paper until only that spot is covered. Leave a bit of soiled paper

Afer a meal is a good time to introduce your Miniature Schnauzer to the paper he is to use for elimination.

If he does right, give plenty of praise.

Even six-week-old puppies can be trained to use the paper.

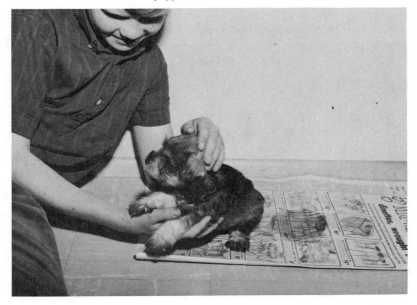

there so that the odor will attract him back. Praise him lavishly if he continues to use the spot. Be sure he knows that you are terribly pleased that he has been such a good dog. Of course, he probably won't know what it's all about for a while, but that's all right; he loves it anyway. Dog scents are available at most petshops to aid you in training your dog should you prefer a more sanitary training method.

As your dog grows up a bit, you will notice that he has to eliminate less and less. Mostly he goes right after naps, meals or play. Now is the time to start housebreaking. Those people who live in apartments have a more difficult job. They must note the signs, pick up the dog, rush to the elevator and race outside to the nearest curb, trying to attach the leash and desperately hoping the dog won't wet in some embarrassing place like the elevator. If you live in a house or garden apartment, your job is considerably easier. As soon as you observe the dog beginning to sniff around or go in circles, grab him and head for the outdoors. Be sure to praise and pat him generously when he cooperates. If you lead him to the same spot each day, the odor will remind him of his job. It's amazing how quickly your dog will learn what all these mad dashes outside mean and obey you willingly. Besides, he generally has to go! This does make it easier. There will

Teach your Miniature Schnauzer to walk on a lead early in his life.

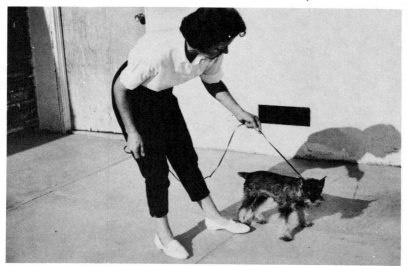

be lapses occasionally. If your dog wets the rug or messes the kitchen floor, immediately chastise him with your voice. Let him know how ashamed you are and how disgusted you feel. Never hit him, never rub his nose in his own mess, and never wait an hour or so before punishment. Dogs have short memories when they are young, and even 15 minutes later he won't have the least idea what you are talking about. If the lapse is just temporary, you are in luck. Occasionally you may have to begin again. This sounds discouraging, but it is the only way to housebreak him properly.

The following hints may be helpful:

1. **Remember that your small puppy has to go quite frequently, and you should be prepared to take him out. You must plan to be home while this basic training is completed.**
2. **Remember to take him out after naps, meals, play, or any excitement (such as strangers in the house or other dogs).**
3. **Praise your dog when he cooperates. Use your voice only when he forgets. And don't expect him to learn the day you begin. Training takes time and the dog must be physically mature.**
4. **If you let your puppy roam the house, you are asking for trouble; keep him confined to one room until you are absolutely sure.**

EARLY TRAINING

COME: This should be the first actual training you give your dog aside from housebreaking, and it is the most important. Once your dog learns to **come** when you call, he is safe from many dangers, and more easily handled.

A puppy should not be forced, so the easiest way to begin training him to **come** is to begin while is he in the house. Just coax him to you, saying **come** in your most wheedling voice. If there is no other big attraction—such as dinner or strangers—who should he come to but you, who else is so willing to play and means warm food and affection? He will sidle up at the sound of your voice, just begging for a pat. And of course you give him one. Repeat this several times a day, using only the one word **come.** Do not keep the lesson up for long and don't punish if he does not obey. Try again, perhaps with a bit of food. When he obeys fairly well, try it outside. Select a quiet spot and call **come.** If he refuses to come to you, take courage in hand and run off. You may fear you will lose him but no puppy can refuse a good chase with his master. If you look around you will see him manfully trying to catch up with you. When he does come up, praise him, pet him, make a big fuss, don't scold him for not obeying immediately.

Once your dog has begun to catch on to the new word in his vocabulary, you can begin adding his name, so he gets used to that. **Come, Kippy** and then **Kippy, come** will teach him his rightful name.

NO and **STOP:** About the same time as you begin teaching your puppy to come to you, you will probably find yourself telling him **no** or **stop.** He's in and out of mischief, and you are spending your days trailing him around to see that he isn't puddling as well as keeping him from chewing up the furniture and turning over the garbage can. If he does get into something he shouldn't, shout a loud **no** or **stop** and then take him away firmly. If he's bent on chewing, give him a rawhide bone and confine him to his room. But be sure and practice consistency. What is forbidden one time should also be forbidden the next, or you may find yourself with a very confused puppy. As a rule it isn't enough just to say **no,** but you must also remove him from the temptation or take the temptation away from him.

Stop can be used when you want the puppy to stop some activity such as biting, barking and growling. Often you will have to close his mouth and hold it shut while you chastise him with **stop** and a most sorrowful look.

LEAD TRAINING

Your dog is housebroken and almost knows when to **come,** and you can begin to think about lead (leash) training. Again, you must have time for training. If you have no spare time, perhaps it would be better to arrange for a professional trainer or school. If you plan to do it yourself, then be prepared to allot sufficient time.

The best type of training collar is a choke collar. This is a collar made of chain, with a ring where the lead is fastened. Slip the collar over the dog's head and attach the chain. A choke collar pulls tighter when you do, and loosens when you let up. It should be removed when not in use.

Tricks can be taught your Miniature Schnauzer. Use trainer's tidbits, available at pet counters, to get your pet to do what you want. Photo by Al Barry of Three Lions, Inc.

Use a sturdy collar so that it does not harm the dog. The lead can be of leather or chain. Be sure it is strong enough if you have an energetic puppy. When you attach the lead to the collar, have it pass over the dog's neck, not under it.

Suppose you collar your dog, attach the lead, and set out for a pleasant walk with him. The first thing he does is refuse to move. Or perhaps he moves too much, rushing off, and bounding in all directions until brought up by the lead. What now? Obviously, you

Dog candy is an excellent treat for Miniature Schnauzers. Photo by Al Barry of Three Lions, Inc.

and this whirling dervish cannot go parading down the street. In the first place, see that you are holding the lead and dog properly. The dog should be on your left side, the lead held in the right hand with your left hand available for extra strength and guidance. If your dog refuses to go with you on a leash, take him home. Let him get very hungry, then attach the leash and lead him to his food. If he associates good things with the collar and lead, he will be more cooperative the next time you plan an outing.

HEEL: What happens if he rushes off, pulling you along? We have seen any number of people being dragged along by their dogs, and this is surely a sign of poor training. If your puppy runs off, jerk the lead with the left hand and then stop, say **come,** and wait for his return. Praise him when he comes back. Sooner or later your dog will see that his wildness only results in stopping the walk altogether and general disapproval. Don't pull, incidentally, just jerk firmly but not unkindly. If you are full of admiration when he does come back, he will do it more willingly. Pretty soon, you can begin to use the word **heel** when he comes and walks at your side. If he stops, jerk him back firmly and say **heel.** If he bounds ahead, do the same thing and praise him when he comes back. Before you know it, he will be marching proudly by your side, the perfect gentleman. Of course, be prepared for little mishaps, such as the local cat, another dog, or an auto which may distract your dog before he has thoroughly mastered the commands to **come** and **heel.** Firmness and kindness should prevail, however.

Once you feel that he has thoroughly learned these lessons, try it off the lead.

Teach your Miniature Schnauzer to walk in the heel position.

Hints to remember:

1. **Never work with your dog on any lesson until he has relieved himself.**

2. **Keep the lessons short. Fifteen minutes at a time is plenty.**

3. **Don't expect a dog to stay at "heel" for the whole walk; after all, he's a dog, isn't he, and a fellow needs a little time to play.**

ADVANCED TRAINING

SIT: Once your dog has learned the above, he is ready for the command to **sit.** You begin by adding the word **down** to his vocabulary. When he comes to you and jumps up, you say **down** and force him down to the ground. Praise him when he obeys. Keep this up until he has learned not to jump up when you begin training.

The next step is **sit.** Stand the dog on your left side with the lead on, and tell him to **sit.** Follow words with action and push his hindquarters down. He may lie down all the way, and then you will just have to haul him up again and push down his hindquarters once more. Should he accidentally or actually begin to **sit,** praise him generously. You can appreciate what a hard lesson this is for him, for all he wants to do is jump up, lap your face and start playing. Repeat the lesson several times a day for short periods. Don't punish; just reward success or partial success with praise.

The command **lie down** can be taught in much the same way. Once the lesson is learned, try it without the lead.

STAY: Your dog now **comes, heels, sits down** and **lies down.** But the minute you leave, he does too! If you can teach him to **stay,** this will prove valuable. Suppose you want him to remain in the car while you shop, or with the baby carriage, or to stay quiet when a friend arrives. He must learn to stay in one place for a short period. Just as with the early lessons, use example and praise. As he learns, increase the scope of the command.

When you first command him to **stay,** sit him down, say **stay,** and then, holding the leash, walk around him or out towards the end of the lead. Of course, he will jump up and follow you. Don't yell at him; simply walk back and force him back into a sitting position, and then say **sit—stay.** You can also use a hand signal. Hold the palm of your hand in front of his nose when you say **sit—**

To begin teaching your Miniature Schnauzer to go over hurdles on command, begin by walking him through the actions while on a lead.

stay. He will learn that as well as the word. After a while, he will get the idea and remain sitting while you walk around him.

When this lesson is learned, you can put the lead on the ground. Perhaps he is again nervous. Hold it with your foot. It won't be too long before you can leave him unattended and walk off. If he bolts after you, no praise, just repeat the whole lesson again. When you think he is sufficiently trained in the sit-stay position, then try distracting him by running off or bouncing a ball under his nose. Each time, if he gets up and starts off, begin again as before. Once the lesson is over and he has performed well, of course you can pat him and tell him how well he has done. Be careful not to pat him as soon as he has remained sitting for a moment, or he will think that the lesson's over.

The authors believe that if your dog is housebroken and can obey the commands to **come, heel, sit, lie down,** and **stay,** he will be completely manageable. You can then teach him tricks if you wish. If you so desire, teach your puppy to beg by propping him in the proper position and encouraging him to repeat this. Do not, however, allow him to use this cute trick to get food from you at the table. If you wish to reward him with a dog biscuit or candy at the time of the trick, fine, but if you feed him while you are eating because he begs so cutely, this cute trick will only become an chronic nuisance.

SPECIAL PROBLEMS

Some dogs, because of indifferent training or lack of training, develop problems which must be cured before they become acute and dangerous. The dog who jumps on people, barks all night, chases cars, and bites or steals food from the table must be retrained.

JUMPING ON PEOPLE: There are several ways to combat this. If your dog will not obey your command to get down and not jump you can try the following: start by telling him **no** and putting him firmly on the floor. If he stays down, pat him. Some trainers advocate that when the dog jumps up you catch him with your knee so he falls back. This is unpleasant enough to stop him. Don't let him get the idea you are hurting him deliberately. As soon as he obeys, praise him.

CHASING CARS: There is no more dangerous and annoying habit for a dog than chasing cars. Dogs have been hit that way, and often in an effort to avoid the dog the driver endangers the lives of

Two of the best rewards in training are praise and affection.

others. The best method is to start early and instill a proper fear of cars. Have another drive a car as you walk your dog along the road. When the car comes along, the driver is to give several loud blasts on the horn. At the same time you jerk your dog over to the side of the road. Repeat this several times, and the dog will instinctively move over to the side when he hears a car.

For the already delinquent dog, more severe methods must be used. The driver of the car can use a water pistol and squirt water at the dog as he jumps out at the car, or the driver can leap out of the car and yell loudly at the dog. Of course, you should be nearby in case the dog becomes frightened enough to attack the man. Once your dog shows that he has learned his lesson, he really deserves a medal! But a piece of dog candy will probably serve just as well.

BARKING: Many people purchase a dog for use as a watchdog. Persons on farms or valuable property, or those who are alone at night, may want a dog to warn them of approaching strangers. In these cases, the dog's bark is an asset. But the dog who barks all night, or barks at everyone regardless of who he is, or never stops barking at familiar people such as the paper boy, or garbage man, should be trained to be silent. Barking is a dog's way of talking and, of course, you don't want to completely muzzle him. But if you live in an apartment or populous neighborhood, a barking dog is very annoying and he often starts other dogs in the area baying. The resulting night-long chorus can cause troublesome relations with non-dog owners, and even some dog owners whose sleep is affected.

Prevention is the best cure, and you can start early after the basic lessons are completed. Begin by leaving your dog alone in his room. If he starts to bark, yell at him or knock loudly at the door. If he persists, go in and look your maddest. You can also be sly and pretend to go away. When he begins to howl, go through the routine again.

BITING: Dogs who bite are potentially dangerous. And dogs who continue to bite can be put away by order of a court if there have been complaints. First and foremost, do not encourage your young puppy to bite people, even playfully (and that is what he is doing when he starts, *just playing*). If he must chew on something, get him some inanimate object such as a toy or a rawhide bone. If he continues to bite, express your disapproval. He may need more severe punishment. Hold his jaw shut until he stops or slap him gently on the muzzle. Be sure to fondle him afterwards if he obeys. If you do not tease your dog, he will be less inclined to bite. A dog doesn't like to be poked or interrupted when he is eating. His instincts may cause him to growl and defend himself. But a dog should not growl at his master; firm treatment will tell him so.

FURNITURE SITTING: Do you come home and find your dog in your favorite chair? Next thing you know, he will have your slippers and your paper too. This is a habit which should be broken, unless you don't mind cleaning bills. Remove the dog firmly. Perhaps you can provide a comfortable spot in the living room for him so he can be with you. If it continues, some trainers advocate setting a little mousetrap under some paper on the chair. The noise will frighten him off. This can be used, but if you are inclined to worry over noses and toes, try a child's squeaky toy or crackly paper.

FOOD STEALING: Dogs who steal food are both impolite and dangerous to themselves. If your dog does take food he may be eating the wrong foods and ruining that careful diet you prepared, or perhaps he may eat a poisonous substance. Train him to take food only from his dinner plate, at his dinner hour, or on special occasions when you offer a treat. A loud **no** when your dog reaches for forbidden food and general disapproval may work, but you can also try pepper on the enticing tidbit.

Begin to teach your dog the broad jump by taking him over it on a lead. Once he has the idea, have him jump on command alone.

Once perfection is attained, lavish praise on the Miniature Schnauzer for a job well done.

Most dogs retrieve naturally, but, if necessary, they can be taught to do so.

Miniature Schnauzer sniffs glove in scent discrimination test, then comes through with flying colors as he returns the object to his trainer.

To teach your dog to retrieve over an obstacle, start by walking him through the actions while on a lead. The next step is to have him do it on command.

A perfect retrieve over the high jump for this Miniature Schnauzer.

Dogs sometimes have other annoying habits which can be cured using much the same methods described above. Kindness and consistency are important and reward for good behavior will reinforce your dog's good habits and discourage bad ones.

SPECIAL TRAINING FOR SHOWING

There are many excellent books on the market describing the type of training you need for showing and obedience trials. One to be highly recommended is the publication **How to Housebreak and Train Your Dog** by Arthur Liebers. This booklet, in addition to basic training, also describes the training needed to qualify for the Obedience Trials of the AKC.

The title of Companion Dog (C.D.) in the Novice Class is awarded if your dog can:

1. Heel on leash
2. Stand for examination by the judge
3. Heel free of the leash
4. Come when called
5. Sit for one minute
6. Sit for three minutes

172

When this hurdle is passed, your dog is ready to earn his C.D.X. (X for Excellent). This requires that he:

1. Heel free
2. Drop on recall
3. Retrieve on flat (ground)
4. Retrieve over an obstacle
5. Broad jump
6. Sit for three minutes
7. Sit for five minutes

He then enters the Utility Class and can compete in tests including scent discrimination, signal exercises, directed jumping, and group exams. The final test is a tracking exercise, and with that he earns his U.D.T. (T for Tracking), the Ph.D. of the Obedience Class.

DOG TRAINING CLASSES

Many dogs are sent by their owners to professional trainers. This is essential when there is no one at home to supervise a dog and teach him his *p's* and *q's*. Or perhaps the dog is undisciplined and active and a trainer is necessary. Another reason might be that you plan to show the dog or place him in Obedience Trials, and want professional help. If your dog has been badly trained or frightened, you may want such a person to straighten him out. Be prepared for fees which may be high. Your veterinarian or breeder can probably recommend a trainer, or you can look through the many dog publications. Be sure when you take the dog home that you receive full instructions on how to handle him and the proper words to use.

CLASSES

Many communities sponsor classes for dogs. The local A.S.P.C.A. or humane society may hold inexpensive classes, or the local dog club may sponsor one. The cost of the classes is generally modest— about $10.00. You will long remember attending the first class of the year in your home town. What bedlam, what a commotion! People and dogs will be pulled all over the place. But by the time the class is under way and in the following weeks, calm, more or less, will reign. You can check with friends or with your veterinarian to see if the classes are effective and the teacher qualified. But don't think that all you will have to do is to attend classes and your

A champion from the kennels of Mrs. S. D. Evans. Photo by Al Barry of Three Lions, Inc.

In scent discrimination tests, the article is taken from the owner's hands with tongs and then placed with other articles by the second party.

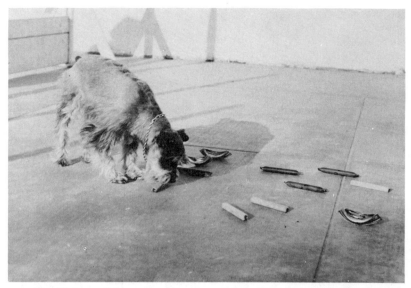
The Miniature Schnauzer sniffs every article until he finds the right one.

dog will be the perfect lady or gentleman. You must be prepared to practice what you *both* have learned when you go home. The advantages of a training class for dogs are that you do obtain the services of a professional who can teach you how to do it, and that the dog becomes accustomed to other dogs and strangers.

Most dogs prefer people to other dogs; they are truly man's companion. But they must learn to respect other dogs and not fight with them. Fights are dangerous both to dogs and the bystanders. If your dog does get into a dog fight, don't step in unless you are prepared to get bitten or scratched. He may be so excited that your dog may not even know you. Cold water from a hose is often effective. If you have guts, you can wade in and grab the most aggressive dog. Hold him tightly by the collar or the throat until he is half choked. He will generally let go. Neighbors who cooperate and keep their dogs in, or penned in runs, rarely have these problems.

SPECIAL ASPECTS OF TRAINING FOR THE MINIATURE SCHNAUZER

Although the Miniature Schnauzer was once used in barnyard and stable as a ratter, we feel that the rat-catching ability of this lovable

After picking the right object, he returns it to his master for a perfect score.

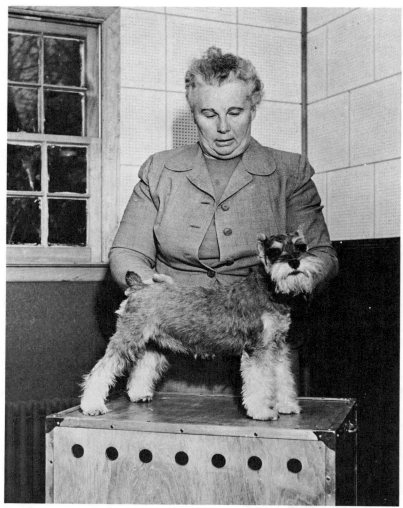

Mrs. S. D. Evans shows how to stack a champion Miniature Schnauzer. Photo by Al Barry of Three Lions, Inc.

little dog is no longer of sufficient importance to justify a discussion of this special problem in training.

Miniature Schnauzers are fine family dogs. They will protect your home and yard, scaring off cats and warning you of strangers. Training should follow the general procedures outlined in this chapter, with only a few special considerations; these are occasioned more by the size of the dog than anything else. Because the Miniature Schnauzer is a small dog, you must be very careful that his collar and lead will not injure him. During training take care, for example, that you don't jerk on the lead too hard. Rough treatment will always do more harm than good.

To summarize . . . training is fundamental if you and your dog are to live together in harmony. A well trained dog is obedient and happy, not cowed or vicious. Keeping him obedient and happy can best be accomplished by training him with kindness, firmness, consistency, and the proper rewards for good behavior.

Chapter X
Kennels, Runs and Bedding

INTRODUCTION

A man's home is his castle, and a dog's home is his kennel. But your dog depends on you to provide him with clean comfortable quarters.

The first thing you must do when your dog arrives is to show him where he lives. This may be a spot in the house or a dog house outside. But it is his own place. And the first rule is that kennels and bedding must be kept clean. Dirty living quarters can harbor many germs, especially worm eggs which are passed on to the dog.

When your Miniature Schnauzer arrives, remember that he is in a strange home, far from his mother, brothers and sisters. You have already decided where he is to stay, indoors or outdoors. Show him his new home, but don't just leave him there and depart, turning off the light or closing the door. He's young, probably frightened and lonely. A little love and affection and time for him to get acquainted and sniff about his bed or kennel and he'll settle in fast enough.

If you live in an apartment, naturally, he will live indoors. If possible, choose a spot that is convenient for the whole family, where the dog can have some privacy. If you live in a house, you have the option of having an indoor or outdoor pet, although most Miniature Schnauzers are kept indoors, where they can be near the family. Generally, only those Miniature Schnauzers intended for use in barn or stable are raised outside. But whatever type of housing you provide for your pet, it must be clean, airy, warm in winter, ventilated in summer and large enough to accommodate your dog.

Keep your kennels spotlessly clean.

Your pet shop has special implements to make cleaning up dog droppings an easy chore.

Your house pet can be taught to use a special area of the yard for his eliminations.

PROFESSIONAL KENNELS

When you consider a kennel for boarding or hospitalization there are certain factors in kennel construction which you should note, to see if the kennel is satisfactory.

A good kennel is large and airy. The ceiling is high, with good ventilation. The kennel contains pens and sleeping areas adequate for the size of dog they accommodate, as well as separate quarters for sick dogs and whelping. Each dog should have his own sleep space, but outdoor pens can be shared for exercise. The kennels should be clean. Some kennels today use wire bottomed pens. These have the advantage of being easier to keep clean and less likely to harbor germs. A wire bottomed pen is made up of two parts: a box for sleeping and an outdoor area for play and exercise. A hinged door provides room to clean and show the dogs. Contrary to what many people think, the wire bottom does not injure the dog's feet.

INDOOR SLEEPING QUARTERS FOR YOUR MINIATURE SCHNAUZER

A Miniature Schnauzer raised inside should have a private place. Sometimes, this may be in the cellar, but only if you are fortunate enough to have a warm dry cellar. Many people use the family room, which has less valuable furniture and rugs than other rooms in the home. Some dog owners make a small cage for their dogs. Of course, your dog's size will also indicate the place he calls his own. It may be just fine for your Miniature Schnauzer to cuddle upon or under your bed at night, but if you also own a Great Dane, this is no place for him, whatever HE may think.

Most people who provide for their dogs indoors purchase a bed. A trip to the neighborhood pet stores will show the number of commercially available sizes and styles. The two major types are wicker and metal, and which one you choose depends on where you plan to put your dog's bed. If he is to be in the kitchen or a bedroom or the family room, the wicker is more attractive. If appearance is no concern, metal is considered sturdier. Be sure that the metal is painted with paint which does not have a lead base. If you are worried about your puppy chewing up the wicker and getting splinters, there is a harmless, bitter tasting preparation on the market which can be rubbed on the wicker and will discourage chewing.

Two types of filling are used for mattresses: cedar shavings and cotton. The mattresses with cedar shavings can be changed, which

A pet shop has all the extras which keep your Miniature Schnauzer happy and healthy, and just as fancy as the dog next door.

may be necessary if you have a small puppy. It may be better, while the dog is young, to provide him with an old blanket which can be chewed to rags. But beware, many dogs become attached to their blanket and won't give it up.

OUTDOOR KENNELS

Most people are concerned with housing a single dog, or two at the most. Outdoor housing can be purchased. If you do buy a dog house, be sure it is solidly constructed, easy to clean and adequately ventilated. It must be large enough! Veterinarians recommend that the sleeping area, your dog's bedroom, be at least two times the width of the grown dog and one and one-half times his height.

Place the kennel in a spot that has some shade as well as sun. If the roof is hinged, you can open it to air the kennel. If possible, place the house a couple of inches off the ground so that moisture and rodents do not affect your dog.

Clean and hose down runs and kennels on a regular basis.

If you don't want your Miniature Schnauzer to sit on furniture, never permit him to do so.

Special car seats for dogs can be purchased at your pet shop.

Your dog house should follow the two-room plan—one room for sleeping, and an entry way. A porch is nice also, so your dog can watch the world go by. If you live in a cold climate, the kennel should be insulated. The hinged roof makes it easy to clean and ventilate.

CAUTION! WHEN YOU PAINT YOUR DOG HOUSE, BE SURE THAT THE PAINT DOES NOT HAVE A LEAD BASE.

Better ventilation will be provided if you slant the roof. And you can also provide a slightly raised curbing at the entry of the bedroom, to keep the bedding in place.

To keep the kennel clean, scrub it with hot water. A mild disinfectant or diluted Lysol can be used to disinfect the kennel. Your dog is proud of his home and not likely to mess it up, but if he has been sick or just wormed, be sure that the kennel is thoroughly scrubbed and disinfected, and the bedding burned.

The best type of bedding for an outdoor kennel is straw or cedar shavings. Cedar shavings are easily purchased in any pet store, and they smell sweet and clean. Your dog may not need bedding in the summer, and just an old sheet or blanket will do. Be sure to change the bedding every so often.

RUNS FOR MINIATURE SCHNAUZERS

If you have a city dog, you naturally will take him for walks on a leash. Both master and dog can get their daily constitutional this way. But in the suburbs or country you may want to provide extra exercise for your dog with a run. One of the problems of the country

Buy your Miniature Schnauzer a dog bed of his own, and chances are he'll not want to sit in your favorite chair.

dog is road safety. Since it is possible to run free—either singly or with groups of other dogs—speeding motorists, wild animals and other natural accidents can endanger his life. The considerate dog owner will provide a place for his dog to exercise when he can't take him out on the leash. The run should be rectangular in shape and as large as you want it to be; 20 × 40 feet or even 8 × 10 feet is plenty large enough. Provide a wire fence several feet high, with a gate fastened with a spring hook.

There are many opinions as to the best flooring for runs and kennels. The one basic principle on which all agree is that the material should be easy to keep clean. Some experts recommend concrete, smoothly troweled and finished. Others say that this harbors worm eggs and is very hard to keep clean. Sand is often recommended, but the same argument is used against sand. Grass, if your run is not permanent, is satisfactory, but you must expect that it will be considerably trampled.

Some dog owners have the kennel and run together. Others put the dog in the run only for exercise. Protect your dog from the hot

Good interior kennels should be light and clean.

For Miniature Schnauzer house pets, you can buy ready-made dog doors that will permit your pet to enter and leave the house at will.

sun by providing some shade if there is no dog house. You can place the run near or under some trees, or construct a platform for protection.

Be sure you provide water also. There is nothing like a fresh drink to cool a fellow off after a hot run around the exercise area. If you do have a run, no matter how large it is, don't leave your pet in for very long stretches. Dogs, like people, get bored, and your dog likes a change of scenery, even if he only goes into the house or his kennel.

Miniature Schnauzers are indoor dogs, mostly, although they love a romp outside. You may not feel it is necessary to have a run for your dog, if he is quite active in the house. Whatever you do, remember that runs and kennels and bedding must be clean and comfortable. This will keep your dog healthier and happier also.

Chapter XI
Grooming and Exercising

GROOMING

Grooming is a matter of habit for both dog and master. Regular grooming should be a pleasurable experience for both; it will be, if your pet is accustomed to being combed and brushed. Start the training of your dog early, be kind but firm, and you will find that he will soon begin to enjoy his grooming sessions.

TRAINING FOR PLEASURABLE GROOMING

The first thing to teach your dog is patience during grooming. Don't let him get away with impatient behavior—after all, who's the boss, anyway?

He must learn to stand quietly while being combed, brushed, trimmed or plucked. This is mostly a matter of starting early in his life. Some breeders begin to brush the pups while they are still in the nest. As a result, they have no difficulty when the pups grow up.

The best place to groom a small dog like the Miniature Schnauzer is on a table, and you will find it easy to lift your small Schnauzer onto the table yourself. The dog's fondness for grooming will simplify your task.

At the start, or if your pet is nervous (or you are!), attach his leash to a hook above the table, which will hold him in place. If your dog is very young, or nervous, start your grooming activities (brushing, combing, etc.) from the rear, so that he can get accustomed to the new noises and sensations.

Have the grooming table become a symbol of a pleasurable affair to your Miniature Schnauzers.

YOUR MINIATURE SCHNAUZER'S COAT

A dog's coat is a direct reflection of his heredity, diet and general health, shown to its best by grooming. Proper care of the coat will assure that it is shiny and free from parasites and coat or skin ailments.

The skin and coat of all dogs have certain general characteristics in common. Dogs' skin contains oil glands (which secrete oil which keeps the coat shining and waterproof), the sebaceous glands (related to hair growth) and some sweat glands.

The sebaceous glands secrete a waxy substance called sebum, which coats the hair as it grows. This is the substance which you may find coating your dog's collar; it sometimes accounts for that "doggy" odor.

The skin of dogs is much like that of human beings, and do not be surprised if your dog occasionally develops dandruff, since the skin continually sheds and renews itself.

Like most other breeds of dogs, Miniature Schnauzers have two coats—a soft undercoat and an outercoat. The Miniature Schnauzer's coat is one of his most attractive features, but it does need careful, regular grooming to look its best. Dogs generally shed once a year, and some seem to shed all year round. We do know that the increasing length of daylight hours in spring is one factor which causes shedding. Dogs who live primarily indoors and are exposed to artificial light may shed more often or even throughout the year. Fortunately, the Miniature Schnauzer rarely sheds, a distinct advantage for apartment dwellers.

COMBING AND BRUSHING

It is a good idea to groom your dog at least once a week. It is better yet if you have the time to do it once a day. This will give your dog a well-groomed look. The Miniature Schnauzer's coat requires both combing and brushing. A suitable sturdy comb which will not break or bend can be obtained in any pet store. When combing the Miniature, be careful to avoid scraping his skin, but be sure that you reach the undercoat. If there are any mats, tease them apart; the use of a little oil will make this task easier. Cutting mats leaves a bald

The coat should be plucked for shows.

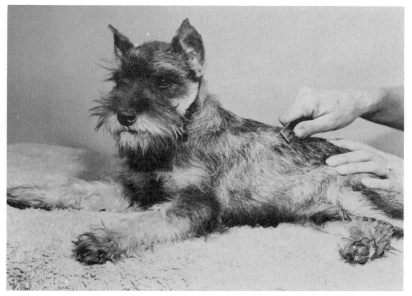

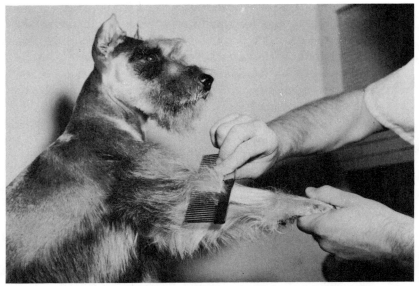

An excellent comb to groom the hair on the Miniature Schnauzer's legs.

Your Miniature Schnauzer's coat will need stripping. See your pet shop for all necessary grooming tools.

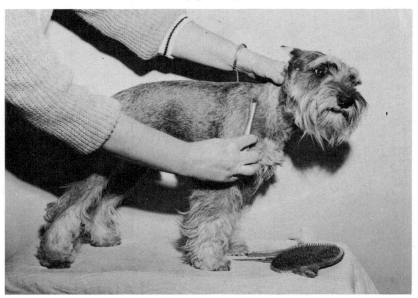

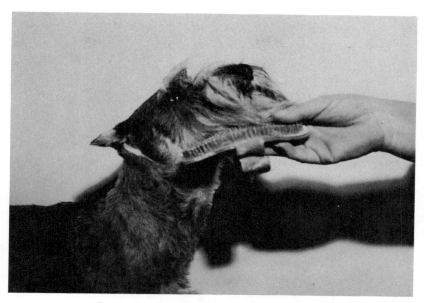

Groom the whiskers regularly with a dog brush.

Use a scissors to cut the path between the eyebrows.

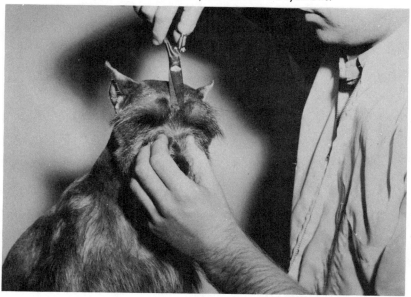

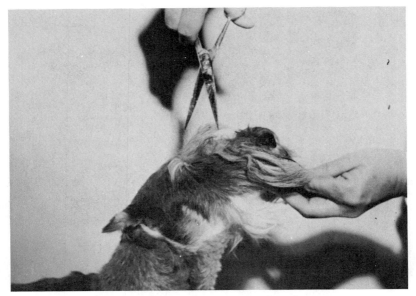

The eyebrows will require trimming, also.

Pull loose hair from ears after clipping to prevent irritation.

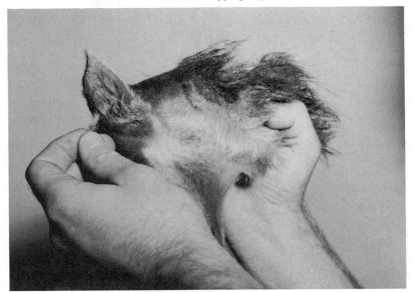

spot which is unsightly. Burrs should also be removed without the use of scissors.

If the coat is not combed regularly, the soft undercoat will grow out over the outercoat, changing its appearance.

Part of the Miniature Schnauzer's appeal is his sturdy and whiskery look. When he is properly trimmed and "put down," as the professionals say, he is one of the handsomest dogs at the dog show or in the neighborhood.

If your dog is to look his best, do not allow him to run in the fields or woods for long periods, as this wears off the leg hair and whiskers. When you are combing him, comb the whiskers forward to the nose, fluff the legs, and then comb the hair straight down. This gives the dog a chubby appearance. A soft mitt or grooming glove may be used to give an extra gloss. You will find that your dog gets much pleasure from this phase of grooming. Both comb and brush should be cleaned after each use (the comb will be helpful in cleaning the brush) and should be stored in the open to air.

THE SPECIAL MINIATURE SCHNAUZER TRIM

When it comes time for a trim, you either go to a professional or do it yourself. The technique and tools for home trims are described below under "Trim."

Trim the whiskers with a scissors.

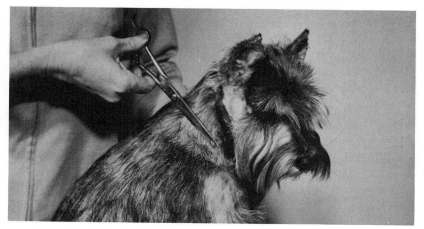

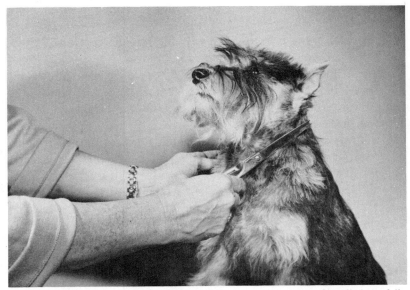

A Miniature Schnauzer will not be afraid of grooming equipment, if handled carefully.

Puppy hair should be hand stripped at about nine weeks. This is accomplished with a stripping knife, which you can buy in a pet store, or your fingers. Pull the hair with the grain, using the knife (see below, "Plucking") or your fingers. Take a little off your puppy each day rather than large amounts all at once. This will be easier on both of you.

PLUCKING

All wire-haired breeds are plucked, not clipped. Clipping spoils the special color and texture of their coats. If a dog with a pepper-and-salt coat is clipped, the color will appear grayish all over.

Plucking can be done by hand, pulling out handfuls of hair, but it is much easier and better to use a regular plucking or stripping knife. This is a flat piece of steel with a handle. The front part has a serrated edge, much like the cutting part of a saw. Holding the handle of the knife in your right hand, with your thumb a short distance from the blade's edge, trap the hair between the edge and the thumb. Then push the hair over the edge, using your thumb, and pull. Let go of the hair which you have loosened and grab another thumbful. If

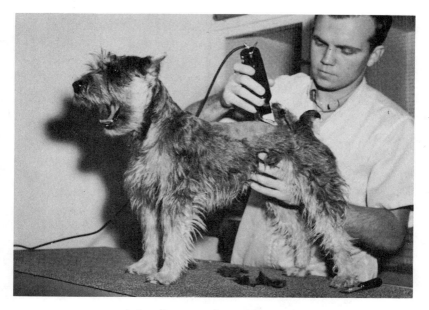

A dog clippers can be used for pet clips.

you do this rapidly, you will soon have removed all the excess soft hair.

This can be time-consuming, and you may want to have a professional do the job. Today there are dog beauty parlors which specialize in dog trims.

If you want to pluck your dog yourself, but are not confident enough to try it, we suggest that you consult with a professional groomer to learn the technique and procedure to follow. You should also become familiar with the necessary equipment.

TRIM

Miniature Schnauzers should be stripped and trimmed about every six months after they have reached maturity. Those which are to be entered in dog shows should be stripped and trimmed nine or ten weeks in advance.

Trim the body closely with the stripping knife. Long hair is left on the front legs and below the hock in back. The head is stripped quite closely from the brows to the base of the skull, and from back of the eyes to the cheeks. The throat and sides of the neck are also

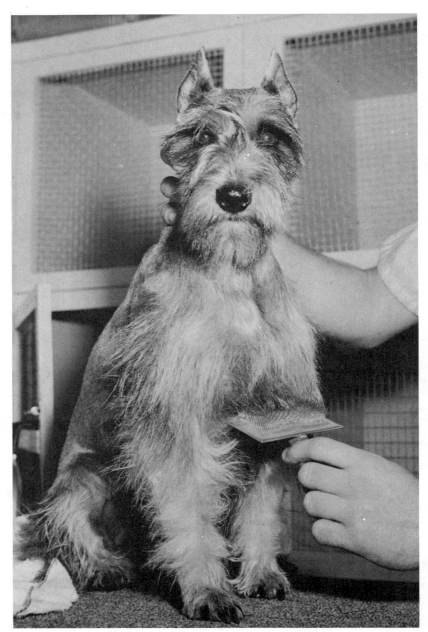

Regular grooming with a dog brush will keep the hard wiry hair in show condition.

trimmed closely and kept free of long hair. Strip the ears and trim the edges with a scissors. The hair from the eyebrows forward should be left long and shaped to fit the head. The body coat is trimmed to ¾ of an inch in length and then kept hard and smooth by proper diet and grooming.

Leave the hair on the thighs a bit longer, but see that they are neat and not scraggly. Trim the legs to look square and sturdy, and then trim the hair between the toes to make the foot look neater, but around the edges trim it only enough to clear the ground. You can finish the job with a scissors, trimming the eyebrows, whiskers and leg furnishings for a neat, tidy, sharp appearance.

After completing the trim, comb and brush the whiskers and then chalk them (see below under "Baths"). Now your dog is properly "put down" and ready to go. It is quite a job to trim a Schnauzer correctly, but the end results—a neat, square, rugged and sturdy looking dog, will delight the whole family.

NAIL CLIPPING

Long nails can force a dog's toes outward and affect his stance permanently if they occur during puppyhood. If you enjoy an

Clip your dog's claws regularly. Use clippers designed specifically for dogs.

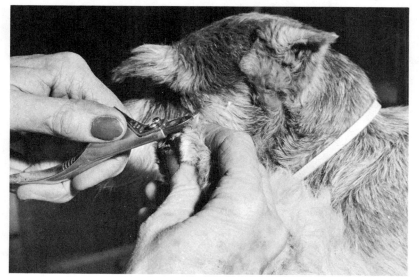

occasional romp with your pet, you will find it safer for both you and your clothing to keep the nails clipped.

Your veterinarian can clip your dog's nails as part of his regular checkup, or you can, with the aid of a pair of nail clippers for dogs, do it yourself. The part you must trim is the hook, that section of the nail which curves down. Be very careful not to cut into the vein running through the nail, as it bleeds profusely. In small pups or light-haired older dogs, the line where the vein begins is easy to spot. With black Miniature Schnauzers, shining a flashlight under the nail can help you spot the vein.

Are you nervous about clipping? Then file the nails. A good file can do an excellent job of shortening nails, or the file can be used to finish the job after the nails are clipped.

If you do cut into the dog's toes, it is not tragic—bandage the foot until the bleeding has stopped and apply a styptic pencil. The bandage helps keep blood from spattering all over the place.

Most people find that their dog's nails need trimming about every two months. But if your dog walks mostly on concrete sidewalks, his nails will wear down naturally and he may never need clipping.

TEETH

A little care goes a long way. Tartar is your dog's worst tooth problem. Dog biscuits and bones made from nylon and animal

You or your veterinarian can remove the tartar from your dog's teeth. Hide and nylon bones will aid in keeping tartar at a minimum.

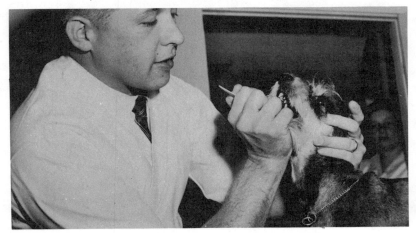

hides are excellent to keep tartar from forming. The authors do not recommend giving meat bones to dogs, even as "toothbrushes." If heavy tartar does form, it can best be removed by your veterinarian.

Sometimes puppy teeth do not fall out on time and must be pulled to make room for the second teeth. Your veterinarian can check for this when your puppy is in for its regular examination.

If your Miniature has "bad breath," check the condition of his mouth and then his diet. There is even a breath deodorizer available at your petshop to make your dog more "sociable."

EARS

It is best to leave a dog's ears alone. More damage is done by probing than by disease. If your dog's ears appear dirty or full of wax, you can clean them out gently with a cotton-tipped swab. But do not thrust the swab far into the ear canal.

Be careful when cleaning a Miniature Schnauzer's ears. Never probe beyond the area you can actually see. Photo by Al Barry of Three Lions, Inc.

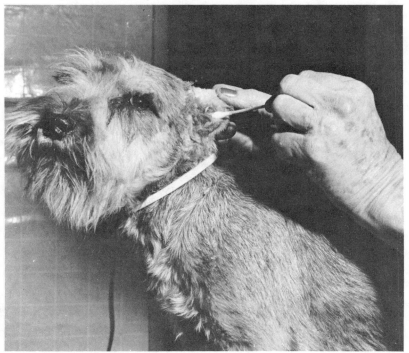

You may at some time see your dog scratching his ears along the ground or shaking his head violently. He may have some sort of irritation, such as canker, in his ear. Check with your veterinarian. He may recommend that you fill the ear with a preparation such as propylene glycol or mineral oil. To do this, put the dog on a table, hold the ear flap so that you can see the ear canal, and pour the oil into the ear until it is filled. Then massage the base of the ear, wiping up the oil that escapes. This treatment dissolves the wax.

Some dogs have hair growing in the ear canal. This is easily removed by using a forceps or pulling it out gently with fingers.

EYES

The eyes rarely need grooming care. If they exude a little matter, it is an easy thing to wipe them out with a piece of moist cotton.

Use cotton dipped in water to clean a dog's eyes.

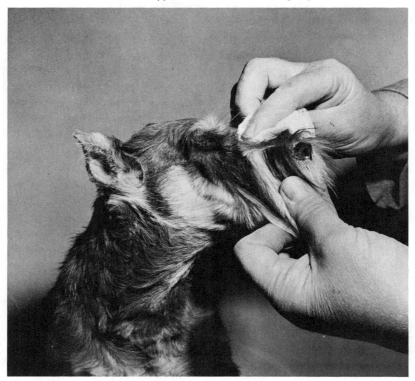

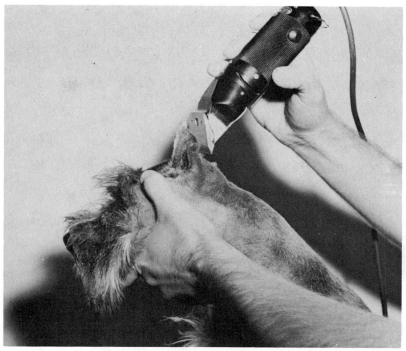
Hold the head steady while you clip the ears.

ANAL GLANDS

The anal glands are two glands situated on either side of the anus. They appear to serve the same purpose as those of a skunk, and they also have an unpleasant odor. If a dog is extremely frightened or the loser in a fight, these glands release their contents. The glands may become enlarged and infected if they are not naturally discharged. To prevent this, they must be emptied from time to time. If your dog begins to drag himself around on his tail, and there is a swollen appearance around the anus, check the glands. If you feel two hard lumps, it's time for action.

To empty the glands, stand the dog in a tub or use a big wad of tissues or cotton, as the liquid you extract is quite smelly. Try not to get any on your hands. With one hand hold the tail up. With the other, using the thumb and middle finger, gently squeeze each lump upward and outward. If this does not empty the glands, they may have to be emptied by a veterinarian.

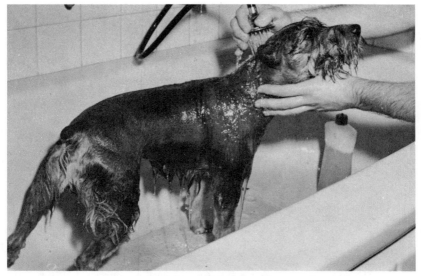

Begin the bath by soaking down the entire dog.

Step two, lather well with dog shampoo.

Step three, rinse and apply shampoo again. Your pet store will have several different brands, including a dry bath.

Step four, give final rinse.

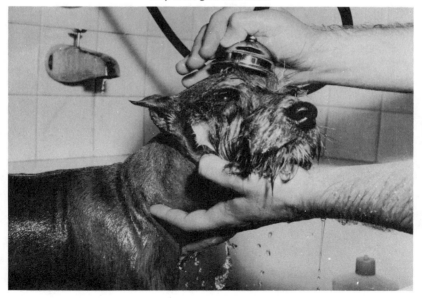

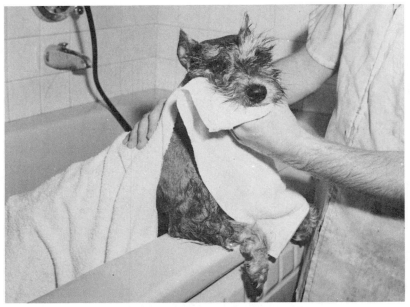

After the rinse, dry him well with a towel.

Many pet shops have special dog-drying machines to speed the bath.

Cage-type dryers are coming into use more and more.

BATHS

To bathe or not to bathe, that is the question. The best rule of thumb is to bathe your dog only when he cannot be cleaned by any other means. If you are regular with combing and brushing, you will find little need to bathe your Miniature Schnauzer, with the exception of whiskers, beard and legs, which require extra attention. You should resort to a bath only if he loves to roll in dirt (a bad habit for many reasons!) or if he gets into paint or tar.

SOAPS

There are many soap preparations on the market to use for your pet. One of the best is a 50% solution of coconut oil which is further diluted with water before use.

The best shampoo is "pet quality" as found in pet stores. "Human

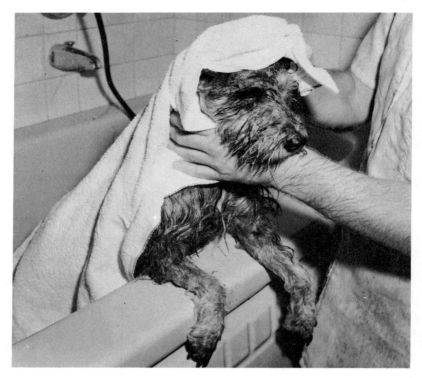

A bath is the only solution to the doggy odor problem.

quality" is not advised, as it may be too harsh for dogs. A new tearless dog shampoo has been developed which eliminates possible eye problems.

Other types of soap are called *dry-bath* soaps and do not need water. They are either powder-based, containing flea killing insecticides, or aerosol spray soaps. The powder types are rubbed in and then brushed out. The sprays are sprayed over the dog and then rubbed and toweled out. Most of the dry baths are excellent but more expensive than regular soaps. Experimentation with various types and brands of commercially available dog soaps will enable you to find the brand which suits your dog best.

TECHNIQUE

Most dogs are best washed in a tub. If your dog won't get into a tub, use a spray attachment which attaches to the faucet. Pour a line of soap down the middle of his back and lather it in. Work it in so that the dog's coat is completely soaped. Rinse and resoap. Then rinse thoroughly so that no trace of soap remains. If you wish, you can then use a dip to bring out the color highlights. Now your dog is ready to be dried, and a good rub is in order. A soft towel is fine, and after that you can step back and admire your pet's clean appearance. When you have finished drying your Miniature Schnauzer, comb his coat down and then place a folded towel over his coat to keep it flat. If it is warm outside, you can let your pet out when he is dry. Be sure that he is *completely* dry before letting him outdoors in chilly weather.

A well-groomed Miniature Schnauzer is a dog that you can be proud of.

BEARD, WHISKERS AND FORELEGS

A Miniature's beard, whiskers and forelegs require special attention. They must be cleaned more frequently than other parts of the body, as they are more easily soiled. For this purpose, we suggest one of the dry-bath soaps or a partial bath, rather than a full bath. Wash

The difference between a groomed and an ungroomed Miniature Schnauzer is adequately illustrated here.

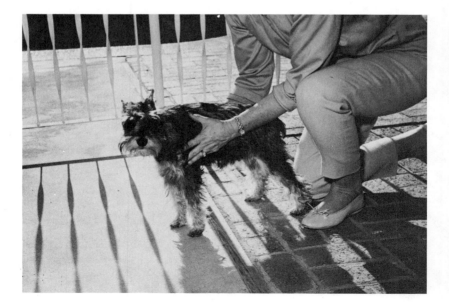

and dry the forelegs fully and fluff them out. When you wash the beard, let the whiskers dry halfway and then rub them with white cleaning chalk (available in your local pet store). Dry thoroughly and brush out the chalk. The whiskers will appear twice as big and very white.

PARASITES

Lice and fleas are fully discussed in the chapter on diseases (Chapter XII), but sometimes routine control of these annoying pests can be part of grooming. If you suspect one of these problems, you can bathe your pet with any of the preparations for flea control on the market. Once you spot fleas, be sure to give the kennel and bedding a good bath too. Many professional kennel owners deflea their dogs' quarters regularly. If you keep both dog and bed free from these pests, chances are he won't suffer from them.

DOGGY ODOR

As your dog gets older, he will smell "doggier." An occasional bath along with a dusting of antiseptic powder for parasites will help. Check his anal glands and teeth and see that his diet is proper, and there will be less odor.

Your dog's collar can also be the source of odor. Take it off when you wash your pet, scrape off the accumulated dirt and wax and clean it with alcohol. Then air it out and oil it well before putting it back on your dog.

SKUNKS

If your dog tangles with a skunk, the skunk will probably be the winner. Unfortunately, both you and the dog are the losers. Don't take off in the other direction when he comes home after one of these encounters. Wash him thoroughly and put him near the heat or out in the sun. The odor will disappear in time. Some people advocate washing the animal in tomato juice, but we have not tried this technique as yet.

PAINTS

The best chemical used to remove paint is kerosene. Rub off the paint as soon as possible with a cloth dipped in kerosene and then wash it off well. Kerosene can burn an animal's skin, so apply it with care.

Keep the dog from chewing on the paint on his fur, as it may contain poisonous substances.

TAR

If the city has been tarring your road, rest assured that your dog will have investigated. He may then come home with tar on his feet or coat. To remove tar, wipe off the tar with kerosene, as above. It may take several treatments.

EXERCISE

Exercise is "doing what comes naturally" for most Miniature Schnauzers. These dogs find plenty of exercise running about the house or following their masters or mistresses.

In earlier days, when the Schnauzer was a younger breed and he was used in barns and stables, that was where he exercised. Chasing rats is no longer either exercise or sport for the Miniature Schnauzer, and he must find his play at home.

If you take your pet for a walk, make sure he's on a lead.

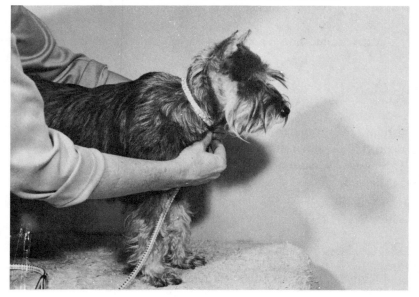

Properly trained Miniature Schnauzers can be exercised in a group.

For the dog living in rural areas, this is no problem; he has plenty or room. But we must help the dog living in crowded urban areas to meet his exercise needs despite the restrictions imposed by life in the city.

The Miniature in the city should be exercised regularly by walking, which he will greatly enjoy. Most towns and cities require that dogs be on a leash when out in the streets, but this should not prevent your dog from getting his full benefit from the walk. He will get the rest in the house or apartment playing with you or the children in the household, or with his toys.

The Miniature in the country can have much more freedom if left to run free for his exercise. You will find, however, that he is more of a homebody, enjoying an occasional walk or romp outdoors. If you do plan for a run, it need not be large (see Chapter X: Kennels, Runs and Bedding).

If you have a puppy you may want playthings to distract him from your shoes or chairs. Most pet stores carry a supply of toys which are safe for dogs. Just be careful with rubber toys; see to it that your energetic puppy does not tear them apart and eat the pieces. Toys are not on his diet list! The safest toys are the natural rawhide "bones" offered at most petshops. Nylon "bones" with natural scents are also very valuable.

If you give your dog adequate exercise and proper grooming, diet, and medical care, he will reward you with "Ohs" and "Ahs" from the neighbors and perhaps even a blue ribbon at the dog show!

Nylabone® is the perfect chewing pacifier for young dogs in their teething stage and even for older dogs to help satisfy that occasional urge to chew. Unlike many other dog bones on the market today, Nylabone® does not splinter or fall apart; it will last indefinitely and as it is used it frills, becoming a doggie toothbrush that cleans teeth and massages gums.

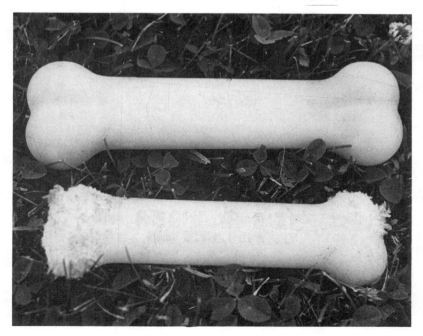

Chapter XII
Diseases and First Aid

The dog is heir to many illnesses, and, as with man, it seems that when one dread form has been overcome by some specific medical cure, another quite as lethal takes its place. It is held by some that this cycle will always continue, since it is Nature's basic way of controlling population.

There are, of course, several ways to circumvent Dame Nature's lethal plans. The initial step in this direction is to put the health of your dog in the hands of one who has the knowledge and equipment to cope competently with canine health problems. We mean, of course, a modern veterinarian. Behind this man are years of study and experience and a knowledge of all the vast research, past and present, which has developed the remarkable cures and artificial immunities that have so drastically lowered the canine mortality rate.

Put your trust in the qualified veterinarian and "beware of Greeks bearing gifts." Beware, too, of helpful friends who say, "I know what the trouble is and how to cure it. The same thing happened to my dog." Home doctoring by unskilled individuals acting upon the advice of unqualified "experts" has killed more dogs than distemper.

Your puppy is constantly exposed to innumerable diseases transmitted by flying and jumping insects, parasites, bacteria, fungus and virus. His body develops defenses and immunities against many of these diseases, but there are many more which we must cure (or immunize him against) if we want him to live his full span.

You are not qualified to treat your dog for many illnesses with the skill or knowledge necessary for success. This book can only give you a resume of modern findings on the most prevalent diseases and illnesses so that you can, in some instances, eliminate them or the causative agent by yourself. Even more important, this chapter will

Healthy Miniature Schnauzers can be yours through proper medical care. Protect your pet through timely inoculations and safeguard him from parasites, also.

help you recognize disease symptoms in time to seek the aid of your veterinarian.

Many illnesses have an incubation period, during the early stages of which the animal himself may not show the symptoms of the disease, but can readily infect other dogs with which he comes in contact. It is readily seen, then, that places where many dogs are gathered together are particularly dangerous to your dog's health.

Parasitic diseases, which we will first consider, must not be taken too lightly, though they are the easiest of the diseases to cure. Great suffering and even death can come to your pup through these parasites if you neglect to realize the importance of both cure and the control of reinfestation.

EXTERNAL PARASITES

The lowly flea is one of the most dangerous insects from which you must protect your dog. It carries and spreads tapeworm, heartworm and bubonic plague, causes loss of coat and weight, spreads skin disease, and brings untold misery to its poor host. These pests are particularly difficult to combat because their eggs—of which they lay thousands—can lie dormant for months, hatching when conditions of moisture and warmth are present. Thus you may think you have rid your dog (and your house) of these devils, only to find that they mysteriously reappear as weather conditions change.

When your dog has fleas, use any good commercial flea powder which contains fresh rotenone. Dust him freely with the powder. It is not necessary to cover the dog completely, since the flea is active and will quickly reach a spot saturated with the powder and die. Rotenone is also fatal to lice. A solution of this drug in pine oil and added to water to be employed as a dip or rinse will kill all insects.
DDT in liquid soap is excellent and long-potent, its effects lasting for as long as a week. Benzene hexachloride, chlordane, and any number of many new insecticides developed for the control of flies are also lethal to fleas. Whatever specific you use should also be used on your dog's sleeping quarters as well as on the animal itself. Repeat the treatment in ten days to eliminate fleas which have been newly hatched from dormant eggs.

TICKS

There are many kinds of ticks, all of which go through similar stages in their life process. At some stage in their lives they all find it necessary to feed on blood. Luckily, these little vampires are fairly easily controlled. The female of the species is much larger than the male, which will generally be found hiding under the female. Care must be taken in the removal of these pests to guard against the mouth parts remaining embedded in the host's skin when the body of the tick is removed. DDT is an effective tick remover. Ether or nail-polish remover, touched to the individual tick, will cause it to relax its grip and fall off the host. The heated head of a match from which the flame has been just extinguished, employed in the same fashion, will cause individual ticks to release their hold and fall from the dog. After veterinary tick treatment, no attempt should be made to remove the pests manually, since the treatment will cause them to drop by themselves as they succumb.

MITES

There are three basic species of mites that generally infect dogs, the demodectic mange mite (red mange), the sarcoptic mange mite

219

(white mange), and the ear mite. Demodectic mange is generally recognized by balding areas on the face, cheeks, and the front parts of the foreleg, which present a moth-eaten appearance. Reddening of the skin and great irritation occurs as a result of the frantic rubbing and scratching of affected parts by the animal. Rawness and thickening of the skin follows. Not too long ago this was a dread disease in dogs, from which few recovered. It is still a persistent and not easily cured condition unless promptly diagnosed and diligently attended to.

Sarcoptic mange mites can infest you as well as your dog. The resulting disease is known as scabies. This disease very much resembles dry dermatitis, or what is commonly called "dry eczema." The coat falls out and the denuded area becomes inflamed and itches constantly.

Ear mites, of course, infest the dog's ear and can be detected by an accumulation of crumbly dark brown or black wax within the ear. Shaking of the head and frequent scratching at the site of the infestation accompanied by squeals and grunting also is symptomatic of the presence of these pests. Canker of the ear is a condition, rather than a specific disease, which covers a wide range of ear infection and which displays symptoms similar to ear mite infection.

All three of these diseases and ear canker should be treated by your veterinarian. By taking skin scrapings or wax particles from the ear for microscopic examination, he can make an exact diagnosis and recommend specific treatment. The irritations caused by these ailments, unless immediately controlled, can result in loss of appetite and weight, and so lower your dog's natural resistance that he is open to the attack of other diseases which his bodily defenses could normally battle successfully.

INTERNAL PARASITES

It seems strange, in the light of new discovery of specific controls for parasitism, that the incidence of parasitic infestation should still be almost as great as it was years ago. This can only be due to lack of realization by the dog owner of the importance of initial prevention and control against reinfestation. Strict hygiene must be adhered to if pups are not to be immediately reinfested. This is particularly true where worms are concerned.

In attempting to rid our dogs of worms, we must not be swayed by amateur opinion. The so-called "symptoms" of worms may be due

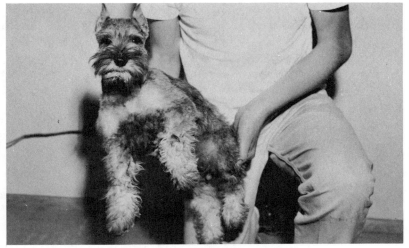

A worm-infested dog will often appear listless.

to many other reasons. We may see the actual culprits in the animal's stool, but even then it is not wise to worm indiscriminately. The safest method to pursue is to take a small sample of your puppy's stool to your veterinarian. By a fecal analysis he can advise just what specific types of worms infest your dog and what drugs should be used to eliminate them.

Do not worm your puppy because you "think" he should be wormed, or because you are advised to do so by some self-confessed "authority." Drugs employed to expel worms can prove highly dangerous to your pup if used indiscriminately and carelessly, and in many instances the same symptoms that are indicative of the presence of internal parasites can also be the signs of some other affliction.

A word here in regard to that belief that garlic will "cure" worms. Garlic is an excellent flavoring agent, favored by gourmets the world over—but—it will not rid your dog of worms. Its only curative power lies in the fact that, should you use it on a housedog who has worms, the first time he pants in your face you will definitely be cured of ever attempting this pseudo-remedy again.

ROUNDWORMS

These are the most common worms found in dogs and can have grave effects upon puppies, which they almost invariably infest.

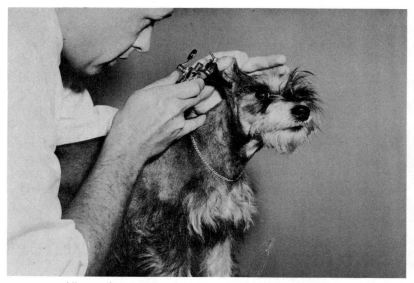

All ear infections should be taken care of by a veterinarian.

Potbellies, general unthriftiness, diarrhea, coughing, lack of appetite, anemia, are the symptoms. They can also cause verminous pneumonia when in the larval stage. Fecal examinations of puppy stools should be made by your veterinarian frequently if control of these parasites is to be constant. Although, theoretically, it is possible for small puppies to be naturally worm free, actually most pups are born infested or contract the parasitic eggs at the mother's teat.

The roundworm lives in the intestine and feeds on the pup's partially digested food, growing and laying eggs which are passed out in the pup's stool to be picked up by him in various ways and so cause reinfestation. The life history of all the intestinal worms is a vicious circle, with the dog the beginning and the end host. This worm is yellowish-white in color and is shaped like a common garden worm, pointed at both ends. It is usually curled when found in the stool. There are several different species of this type of worm. Some varieties are more dangerous than others. They discharge toxin within the pup, and the presence of larvae in important internal sections of the pup's body can cause death.

The two drugs most used by kennel owners for the elimination of roundworms are N-butyl-chloride and tetrachloroethylene, but there are a host of other drugs, new and old, that can also do the job efficiently. With most of the worm drugs, give no food to the dog for twenty-four hours, or in the case of puppies, twenty hours, previous to the time he is given the medicine. It is absolutely essential that this starvation limit be adhered to, particularly if the drug used is tetra-chloroethylene, since the existence of the slightest amount of food in the stomach or intestine can cause death. One tenth c.c. to each pound of the animal's weight is the dosage for tetrachloroethylene, followed in one hour with a milk-of-magnesia physic, *never* an oily physic. Food may be given two hours later.

N-butyl-chloride is less toxic if the pup has eaten some food during the supposed starvation period. The dosage is one c.c. for every ten pounds of the weight of the dog. Any safe physic may be administered an hour later, and the pup fed within two hours afterward. Large doses of this drug can be given grown dogs without danger, and will kill whipworms as well as roundworms. A second treatment should follow in two weeks. The effect of N-butyl-chloride is cumulative; therefore, when a large dosage is necessary, the total amount to be given can be divided into many small doses administered, one small dose at a time, over a period of hours. The object of this procedure is to prevent the dog from vomiting up the drug, which generally occurs when a large dose is given all at once. This method of administering the drug has been found to be very effective.

HOOKWORMS

These tiny leeches who live on the blood of your dog, which they get from the intestinal walls, cause severe anemia, groaning, fits, diarrhea, loss of appetite and weight, rapid breathing, and swelling of the legs. The same treatment used to eradicate roundworms will also expel hookworms.

Good food is essential for quick recovery, with added amounts of liver and raw meat incorporated in the diet. Blood transfusions are often necessary if the infestation has been heavy. If one infestation follows another, a certain degree of immunity to the effects of the parasite seems to be built up by the dog. A second treatment should be given two weeks following the initial treatment.

WHIPWORMS

These small, thin whiplike worms are found in the intestines and the caecum. Those found in the intestines are reached and killed by

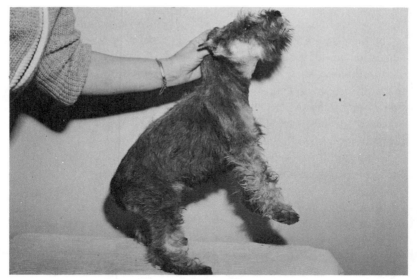
Never lift a healthy Miniature Schnauzer in this way.

the same drugs used in the eradication of roundworms and hookworms. Most worm medicines will kill these helminths if they reach them, but those which live in the caecum are very difficult to reach. They exude toxins which cause debilitation, anemia, and allied ills, and are probably a contributing factor in lowering the resistance to the onslaught of other infections. The usual symptoms of worm infestation are present.

N-butyl-chloride, in dosage three times greater than the roundworm dosage, appears to be quite effective in reaching the caecum and ridding the grown dog of most of these pests. The drug is to be given following the twenty-four hour period of fasting. Administration of an anti-emetic is generally indicated to keep the dog from disgorging the drug.

Hydrogen peroxide administered as an enema is highly effective but very dangerous, and should be applied only by expert hands.

TAPEWORMS

Tapeworms are not easily diagnosed by fecal test, but are easily identified when visible in the dog's stool. The worm is composed of two distinct parts, the head and the segmented body. It is pieces of the segmented body that we see in the stools of the dog. They are usually pink or white, and flat. The common tapeworm, which is most prevalent in our dogs, is about eighteen inches long, and the larvae are carried by the flea. The head of the worm is smaller than a pinhead and attaches itself to the intestinal wall. Contrary to general belief, the puppy infested with tapeworms does not possess an enormous appetite—rather it fluctuates from good to poor. The animal shows the general signs of worm infestation. Often he squats and drags his hindquarters on the ground. This is due to tapeworm larvae moving and wriggling in the lower bowels. One must be careful in diagnosing this symptom, as it may also mean that the dog is suffering from distended anal glands.

Arecolene is an efficient expeller of tapeworms. Dosage is approximately one-tenth grain for every fifteen pounds of the dog's weight, administered after twenty hours of fasting. Nemural is also widely used. One pill for every eight pounds of body weight is given in a small amount of food after twelve hours of starvation. No worm medicine can be considered 100 percent effective in all cases. If one drug does not expel the worms satisfactorily, then another must be tried.

HEARTWORM

This villain inhabits the heart and is the most difficult to treat. The worm is about a foot long and literally stuffs the heart of the affected animal. It is prevalent in the southern states and has long been the curse of sporting-dog breeds. The worm is transmitted principally through the bite of an infected mosquito, which can fly from an infected southern canine visitor directly to your dog and do its dire deed.

The symptoms are: fatigue, gasping, coughing, nervousness, and sometimes dropsy and swelling of the extremities. Treatment for heartworms definitely must be left in the hands of your veterinarian. A wide variety of drugs are used in treatment. The most commonly employed are the arsenicals, antimony compounds, and caracide. Danger exists during cure when dying adult worms move to the lungs, causing suffocation, or when dead adults, in a heavily infested dog, block the small blood vessels in the heart muscles. The invading microfilariae are not discernible in the blood until nine months following introduction of the disease by the bite of the carrier mosquito.

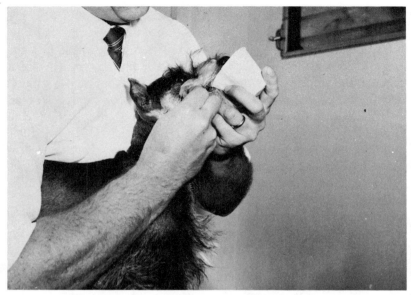

Worm your dog according to your veterinarian's direction.

In an article on this subject in *Field and Stream* magazine, Joe Stetson describes a controlled experiment in which caracide was employed in periodic treatments as a preventive of heartworm. The experiment was carried out over a period of eighteen months, during which time the untreated dogs became positive for heartworm and eventually died. A post mortem proved the presence of the worm. The dogs that underwent scheduled prophylaxis have been found, by blood test, to be free of circulating microfilariae and are thriving.

COCCIDIOSIS

This disease is caused by a single-celled protozoa. It affects dogs of all ages, but is not dangerous to mature animals. When puppies become infected by a severe case of coccidiosis, it very often proves fatal, since it produces such general weakness and emaciation that the puppy has no defense against other invading harmful organisms. Loose and bloody stools are indicative of the presence of this disease, as is loss of appetite, weakness, emaciation, discharge from the eyes, and a fever of approximately 103 degrees. The disease is contracted directly or through flies that have come from infected quarters. Infection seems to occur over and over again, limiting the puppy's chance of recovery with each succeeding infection. The duration of the disease is about three weeks, but new infestations can stretch this period of illness on until your puppy has little chance to recover. Strict sanitation and supportive treatment of good nutrition—utilizing milk, fat, kaopectate, and bone ash with added dextrose and calcium—seem to be all that can be done in the way of treatment. Force feed the puppy if necessary. The more food that you can get into him to give him strength until the disease has run its course, the better will be his chances of recovery. Specific cures have been developed in other animals and poultry, but not as yet in dogs.

SKIN DISEASES

Diseases of the skin in dogs are many, varied, and easily confused by the puppy owner. All skin afflictions should be immediately diagnosed and treated by your veterinarian. Whatever drug is prescribed must be employed diligently, and in quantity, and generally long after surface indications of the disease have ceased to exist. A surface cure may be attained, but the infection remains buried deep in the hair follicles or skin glands, to erupt again if treatment is suspended too soon. Contrary to popular belief, diet, if well balanced and complete, is seldom the cause of skin disease.

Eczema

The word "eczema" is a much-abused word, as is the word "dermatitis." Both are used with extravagance in the identification of various forms of skin disorders. We will concern ourselves with the two most prevalent forms of so-called eczema, namely wet eczema and dry eczema. In the wet form, the skin exudes moisture and then scabs over, due to constant scratching and biting by the dog at the site of infection. The dry form manifests itself in dry patches which irritate and itch, causing great discomfort to the dog. In both instances the hair falls out and the spread of the disease is rapid. The cause of these diseases is not yet known, though many are thought to be originated by various fungi and aggravated by allergic conditions. The quickest means of bringing these diseases under control is through the application of a good skin remedy often combined with a fungicide, which your veterinarian will prescribe. An over-all dip,

227

employing specific liquid medication, is beneficial in many cases and has a continuing curative effect over a period of days.

Ringworm

This infection is caused by a fungus and is highly contagious to humans. In the dog it generally appears on the face as a round or oval spot from which the hair has fallen. Ringworm is easily cured by the application of iodine and glycerine (50 per cent of each ingredient) or a fungicide liberally applied. The new antibiotic Malucidin eliminates ringworm quickly and effectively.

Acne

Your puppy will frequently display small eruptions on the soft skin of his belly. These little pimples rupture and form a scab. The rash is caused by inflammation of the skin glands and is not a serious condition. Treatment consists of washing the affected area with alcohol or witch hazel, followed by the application of a healing lotion or powder.

Hookworm Larvae Infection

The skin of your pup can become infected from the eggs and larvae of the hookworm acquired from a muddy hookworm-infested run. The larvae becomes stuck to his coat with mud and burrow into the skin, leaving ugly raw red patches. One or two baths in warm water to which an antiseptic has been added usually cures the condition quickly.

DEFICIENCY DISEASES

These diseases, or conditions, are caused by dietary deficiencies or some condition which robs the diet of necessary ingredients. Anemia, a deficiency condition, is a shortage of hemoglobin. Hookworms, lice, and any disease that depletes the system of red blood cells, are contributory causes. A shortage or lack of specific minerals or vitamins in the diet can also cause anemia. Not so long ago, rickets was the most common of the deficiency diseases, caused by a lack of one or more of the dietary elements—vitamin D, calcium, and phosphorus. There are other types of deficiency diseases originating in dietary inadequacy and characterized by unthriftiness in one or more phases. The cure exists in supplying the missing food factors to the diet. Sometimes, even though all the necessary dietary elements are present in the food, some are destroyed by improper feeding procedure. For example, a substance in raw eggs, avertin, destroys biotin, one of the B-complex group of vitamins. Cooking will destroy the avertin in the egg white and prevent a biotin deficiency in the diet.

BACTERIAL DISEASES

In this group we find leptospirosis, tetanus, pneumonia, strep infections and many other dangerous diseases. The mortality rate is generally high in all of the bacterial diseases, and treatment should be left to your veterinarian.

Leptospirosis

Leptospirosis is spread most frequently by the urine of infected dogs, which can infect for six months or more after the animal has recovered from the disease. Rats are the carriers of the bacterial agent which produces this disease. A puppy will find a bone upon which an infected rat has urinated, chew the bone, and become infested with the disease in turn. Leptospirosis is primarily dangerous in the damage it does to the kidneys. Complete isolation of affected individuals to keep the disease from spreading and rat control are the chief means

Broken bones can mend properly if set by the competent hands of a veterinarian.

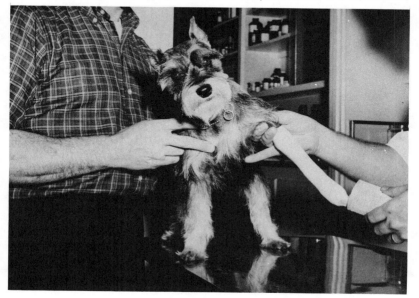

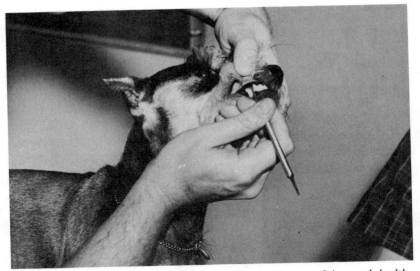

Your veterinarian is skilled to take care of most of your Miniature Schnauzer's health needs.

of prevention. Also, newly developed vaccines may be employed by your veterinarian as a preventive measure. Initial diagnosis is difficult, and the disease has generally made drastic inroads before a cure is effected. It has been estimated that fully 50 percent of all dogs throughout the world have been stricken with leptospirosis at one time or another and that in many instances the disease was not recognized for what it was. The disease produced by *Leptospira* in the blood of humans is known as Weil's disease.

Tetanus

Lockjaw bacteria produce an exceedingly deadly poison. The germs grow in the depths of a sealed-over wound where oxygen cannot penetrate. To prevent this disease, every deep wound acquired by your dog should be thoroughly cleansed and disinfected, and an antitoxin given the animal. Treatment follows the same general pattern as prevention. If the jaw locks, intravenous feeding must be given.

Strep throat

This is a very contagious disease caused by a specific group of bacteria labeled "streptococcus." Characteristic of this disease is the high temperature that accompanies infection (104 to 106 degrees).

Other symptoms are loose stool at the beginning of the disease and a slight optic discharge. The throat becomes intensely inflamed, swallowing is difficult, and the glands under the ears are swollen. Immunity is developed by the host after the initial attack.

Tonsillitis

Inflammation of the tonsils can be either of bacterial or virus origin. It is not a serious disease in itself, but is often a symptom of other diseases. Tonsillitis is not to be confused with strep throat, which is produced by an entirely different organism. The symptoms of tonsillitis are enlarged and reddened tonsils, poor appetite, vomiting, and optic discharge. The disease usually runs its course in from five to seven days. Penicillin, aureomycin, terramycin, chloromycetin, etc., have been used with success in treatment.

Pneumonia

Pneumonia is a bacterial disease of the lungs of which the symptoms are poor appetite, optic discharge, shallow and rapid respiration. Affected animals become immune to the particular type of pneumonia from which they have recovered. Oral treatment utilizing antibiotic or sulfa drugs, combined with a pneumonia jacket of cloth or cotton padding wrapped around the chest area, seems to be standard treatment.

VIRAL DISEASES

The dread viral diseases are caused by the smallest organisms known to man. They live in the cells and often attack the nerve tissue. The tissue thus weakened is easily invaded by many types of bacteria. Complications then set in, and it is these accompanying ills which usually prove fatal. The secondary infections can be treated with several of the "wonder" drugs, and excellent care and nursing is necessary if the stricken animal is to survive. Your veterinarian is the only person qualified to aid your pup when a viral disease strikes. The diseases in this category include distemper, infectious hepatitis, rabies, kennel cough, housedog disease, and primary encephalitis— the latter actually inflammation of the brain, a condition characterizing several illnesses, particularly those of viral origin.

Distemper

Until recently a great many separate diseases had been lumped under the general heading of distemper. In the last few years modern science has isolated a number of separate diseases of the distemper complex, such as infectious hepatitis, hard-pad disease, influenza, and primary encephalitis, which had been diagnosed as distemper. Thus, with more accurate diagnosis, great strides have been made in conquering not only distemper, but these other, allied diseases. Distemper (Carre) is now rare, due to successful methods of immunization, but any signs of illness in an animal not immunized may be the beginning of the disease. The symptoms are so similar to those of various other diseases that only a trained observer can diagnose correctly. Treatment consists of the use of drugs to counteract complications arising from the invasion of secondary diseases and in keeping the stricken animal warm, well fed, comfortable and free from dehydration until the disease has run its course. In many instances, even if the pup gets well, he will be left with some dreadful souvenir of the disease which will mar him for life. After-effects are common in most of the diseases of the distemper complex.

The tremendous value of immunization against this viral disease cannot be exaggerated. Except for the natural resistance your animal carries against disease, it is the one means of protection you have against this killer. There have been various methods of immunization developed in the last several years, but it would seem that the most recently favored is the avianized vaccine (or chick embryo-adapted vaccine). There are reasonably sure indications that this avianized vaccine protects against hard-pad disease and primary encephalitis as well as distemper. Injections can be given at any age, even as early as six or eight weeks, with a repeat dosage at six months of age. It does not affect the tissues, nor can it cause any ill effects to other dogs who come in contact with the vaccinated animal.

Infectious hepatitis

This disease attacks dogs of all ages, but is particularly deadly to puppies. We see young puppies in the nest, healthy, bright and sturdy; suddenly they begin to vomit, and the next day they are dead of infectious hepatitis—it strikes that quickly. The disease is almost impossible to diagnose correctly, and there is no known treatment that will cure it. Astute authorities claim that if an afflicted dog survives three days after the onslaught of the disease he will, in all probability, completely recover. Research has given us a vaccine that affords safe and effective protection against infectious hepatitis.

Rabies

This is the most terrible of diseases, since it knows no bounds. It is transmissible to all kinds of animals and birds, including the superior animal, man. To contract this dread disease, the dog must be bitten by a rabid animal or the rabies virus must enter the body through a broken skin surface. The disease incubation period is governed by the distance of the virus point of entry to the brain. The closer the point of entry is to the brain, the quicker the disease manifests itself. We can be thankful that rabies is not nearly as prevalent as is supposed by the uninformed. Restlessness, excitability, perverted appetite, character reversal, wildness, drowsiness, loss of acuteness of senses, (and of feeling, in some instances) foaming at the mouth, and many other lesser symptoms come with the onslaught of this disease. Diagnosis by trained persons of a portion of the brain is conceded to be the only way of determining whether an animal died of rabies or of one of the distemper complex diseases. Very little has been done in introducing drugs or specifics that can give satisfaction in combating this disease; perhaps evaluation of the efficacy of such products is almost impossible with a disease so rare and difficult to diagnose.

In 1948 an avianized, modified live virus vaccine was reported, and is being used in clinical trials with some success. Quarantine, such as that pursued in England, even of six months' duration, is still not the answer to the rabies question, though it is undeniably effective. It is, however, not proof positive. Recently a dog on arriving in England was held in quarantine for the usual six months. The day before he was to be released to his owners, the attendant noticed that he was acting strangely. He died the next day. Under examination his brain showed typical inclusion bodies, establishing the fact that he had died of rabies. This is a truly dangerous disease that can bring frightful death to animal or man. With an effective way of immunization known and recommended by authoritative sources, it should be the duty of every dog owner to protect his dog, himself, his family, and neighbors from even the slight risk that exists of contracting rabies by taking immediate advantage in this form of protection.

FITS

Fits in dogs are symptoms of diseases rather than illness itself. They can be caused by the onslaught of any number of diseases, including worms, distemper, epilepsy, primary encephalitis, poisoning, etc. Running fits can also be traced to dietary deficiencies. The underlying reason for the fits, or convulsions, must be diagnosed by your veterinarian and the cause treated.

DIARRHEA

Diarrhea, which is officially defined as watery movements occurring eight or more times a day, is often a symptom of one of many other diseases. But, if on taking your dog's temperature, you find there is no fever, it is quite possible the condition has been caused by either a change of diet, of climate or water, or even by a simple intestinal disturbance. A tightening agent such as Kaopectate should be given. Water should be withheld and corn syrup, dissolved in boiled milk, substituted to prevent dehydration in the patient. Feed hard-boiled eggs, boiled milk, meat, cheese, boiled white rice, cracker, kibbles, or dog biscuits. Add a tablespoonful of bone ash (not bone meal) to the diet. If the condition is not corrected within two or three days, if there is an excess of blood passed in the stool, or if signs of other illness become manifest, don't delay a trip to your veterinarian.

CONSTIPATION

If the dog's stool is so hard that it is difficult for him to pass it and he strains and grunts during the process, then he is obviously constipated. The cause of constipation is diet. Bones and dog biscuits, given abundantly, can cause this condition, as can any of the items of diet mentioned above as treatment for diarrhea. Chronic constipation can result in hemorrhoids which, if persistent, must be removed by surgery. The cure for constipation and its accompanying ills is the introduction of laxative food elements into the diet. Stewed tomatoes, buttermilk, skim milk, whey, bran, alfalfa meal, and various fruits can be fed and a bland physic given. Enemas can bring quick relief. Once the condition is rectified, the dog should be given a good balanced diet, avoiding all types of foods that will produce constipation.

EYE AILMENTS

The eyes are not only the mirror of the soul, they are also the mirror of many kinds of disease. Discharge from the eyes is one of the many symptoms warning of most internal viral, parasitic, and bacterial diseases. Of the ailments affecting the eye itself, the most usual are: glaucoma, which seems to be a hereditary disease; pink eye, a strep infection; cataracts; opacity of the lens in older dogs; corneal opacity, such as follows some cases of infectious hepatitis; and teratoma. Mange, fungus, inturned lids, and growths on the lid are other eye ailments. The wise procedure is to consult your veterinarian for specific treatment.

When the eyes show a discharge from reasons other than those that can be labeled "ailment", such as irritation from dust, wind, or sand, they should be washed with warm water on cotton or a soft cloth. After gently washing the eyes, an ophthalmic ointment combining a mild anesthetic and antiseptic can be utilized. Butyl sulphate, 1 percent yellow oxide of mercury, and 5 percent sulphathiazole ointment are all good. Boric acid seems to be falling out of favor as an opthalmic antiseptic. The liquid discharged by the dog's tear ducts is a better antiseptic, and much cheaper.

ANAL GLANDS

If your male dog consistently drags his rear parts on the ground or bites this area, the cause is probably impacted anal glands. These glands, which are located on each side of the anus, should be periodically cleared by squeezing. The job is not a nice one, and can be much more effectively done by your veterinarian. Unless these glands are kept reasonably clean, infection can become housed in this site, resulting in the formation of an abscess which will need surgical care. Dogs that get an abundance of exercise seldom need the anal glands attended to.

The many other ailments which your dog is heir to, such as cancer, tumors, rupture, heart disease, fractures, and the results of accidents, must all be diagnosed and tended to by your veterinarian. When you go to your veterinarian with a sick dog, always remember to bring along a sample of his stool for analysis. Many times samples of his urine are needed, too. Your veterinarian is the only one qualified to treat your dog for disease, but protection against disease is to a great extent in the hands of the dog owner. If those hands are capable, a great deal of pain and misery for both dog and owner can be eliminated. Death can be cheated, investment saved, and veterinary bills kept to a minimum. A periodic health check by your veterinarian is a wise investment.

ADMINISTERING MEDICATION

Some people seem to have ten thumbs on each hand when they attempt to give medicine to their dog. They become agitated and approach the task with so little sureness that their mood is communicated to the patient, increasing the difficulties. Invite calmness and quietness in the patient by emanating these qualities yourself. Speak to the animal in low, easy tones, petting him slowly, quieting him down in preparation. The administration of medicine should be made without fuss and as though it is some quiet and private new game between you and your dog.

At the corner of your dog's mouth there is a lip pocket perfect for the administering of liquid medicine if used correctly. Have the animal sit, then raise his muzzle so that his head is slanted upward looking toward the sky. Slide two fingers in the corner of his mouth where the upper and lower lip edges join, pull gently outward, and you have a pocket between the cheek flesh and the gums. Into this pocket pour the liquid medicine slowly. Keep his head up, and the liquid will run from the pocket into his throat and he will swallow it. Continue this procedure until the complete dose has been given. This will be easier to accomplish if the medicine has been spooned into a small bottle. The bottle neck, inserted into the lip pocket, is tipped, and the contents will slowly run down his throat.

To give pills or capsules, the head of the patient must again be raised with muzzle pointing upward. With one hand, grasp the cheeks of the pup just behind the lip edges where the teeth come together on the inside of the mouth. With the thumb on one side and the fingers on the other, press inward as though squeezing. The lips are pushed against the teeth, and the pressure of your fingers forces the mouth open. The dog will not completely close his mouth, since doing so would cause him to bite his lips. With your other hand, insert the pill in the patient's mouth as far back on the base of the tongue as you can, pushing it back with your second finger. Withdraw your hand quickly, allow the dog to close his mouth, and hold it closed with your hand, but not too tightly. Massage the dog's throat and watch for the tip of his tongue to show between his front teeth, signifying the fact that the capsule or pill has been swallowed.

In taking your dog's temperature, an ordinary rectal thermometer is adequate. It must be first shaken down, then dipped in vaseline, and inserted into the rectum for approximately three-quarters of its length. Allow it to remain there for no less than a full minute, restraining the dog from sitting during that time. When withdrawn, it should be wiped with a piece of cotton, read, then washed in alcohol—never hot water. The arrow on most thermometers at 98.6 degrees indicates normal human temperature and should be disregarded. Normal temperature for your grown dog is $101\frac{1}{2}$ degrees; normal dog temperature varies between $101\frac{1}{2}$ and 102 degrees. Excitement can raise the temperature, so it is best to take a reading only when the dog is calm.

In applying an ophthalmic ointment to the eye, simply pull the lower lid out, squeeze a small amount of ointment into the pocket thus produced, and release the lid. The dog will blink, and the ointment will spread over the eye.

Should you find it necessary to give your dog an enema, employ an ordinary human-size bag and rubber hose. Simply grease the catheter with vaseline and insert the hose well into the rectum. The bag should be held high for a constant flow of water. A bottle of warm soapy water or plain water with a tablespoonful of salt makes an efficient enema for a big dog. Puppies need proportionately less.

FIRST AID

Emergencies quite frequently occur which make it necessary for you to care for the dog yourself until veterinary aid is available. Quite often emergency help by the owner can save the pup's life or lessen the chance of permanent injury. A badly injured animal, blinded to all else but abysmal pain, often reverts to the primitive, wanting only to be left alone with his misery. Injured, panic-stricken, not recognizing you, he might attempt to bite when you wish to help him. Under the stress of fright and pain, this reaction is normal in animals. A muzzle can easily be slipped over his foreface, or a piece of bandage or strip of cloth can be fashioned into a muzzle by looping it around the dog's muzzle, crossing it under the jaws, and bringing the two ends around in back of the dog's head and tying them. Snap a leash onto his collar as quickly as possible to prevent him from running away and hiding. If it is necessary to lift him, grasp him by the neck, getting as large a handful of skin as you can, as high up on the neck as possible. Hold tight and he won't be able to turn his head far enough around to bite. Lift him off the ground by the hold you have on his neck, encircle his body with your other arm, and support him or carry him.

Every dog owner should have handy a first-aid kit specifically for the use of his dog. It should contain a thermometer, surgical scissors, rolls of three-inch and six-inch bandage, a roll of one-inch adhesive tape, a package of surgical cotton, a jar of vaseline, enema equipment, bulb syringe, ten c.c. hypodermic syringe, flea powder, skin remedy, tweezers, ophthalmic ointment, paregoric, Kaopectate, peroxide of hydrogen, merthiolate, Army Formula Foot Powder, alcohol, ear remedy, aspirin, milk of magnesia, castor oil, mineral oil, and dressing salve.

Here are two charts for your reference, one covering general first-aid measures and the other a chart of poisons and antidotes.

FIRST-AID CHART

Emergency	Treatment	Remarks
Accidents	Automobile, treat for shock. If gums are white, indicates probable internal injury. Wrap bandage tightly around body until it forms a sheath. Keep very quiet until veterinarian comes.	Call veterinarian immediately.
Bee stings	Give paregoric or aspirin to ease pain. If in state of shock, treat for same.	Call veterinarian for advice.
Bites (animal)	Tooth wounds—area should be shaved and antiseptic solution flowed into punctures, with eye dropper. Iodine, merthiolate, etc., can be used. If badly bitten or ripped, take dog to your veterinarian for treatment.	If superficial wounds become infected after first aid, consult veterinarian.
Bloat	Stomach distends like a balloon. Pierce stomach wall with hollow needle to allow gas to escape. Follow with stimulant—2 cups of coffee.	
Burns	Apply strong, body heat strained tea to burned area, followed by covering of vaseline.	Unless burn is very minor, consult veterinarian immediately.
Broken bones	If break involves a limb, fashion splint to keep immobile. If ribs, pelvis, shoulder, or back involved, keep dog from moving until professional help comes.	Call veterinarian immediately.

Choking	If bone, wood, or any foreign object can be seen at back of mouth or throat remove with fingers. If object can't be removed or is too deeply imbedded or too far back in throat, rush to veterinarian immediately.	
Cuts	Minor cuts: allow dog to lick and cleanse. If not within his reach, clean cut with peroxide, then apply merthiolate. Severe cuts: apply pressure bandage to stop bleeding—a wad of bandage over wound and bandage wrapped tightly over it. Take to veterinarian.	If cut becomes infected or needs suturing, consult veterinarian.
Dislocations	Keep dog quiet and take to veterinarian at once.	
Drowning	Artificial respiration. Lay dog on his side, push with hand on his ribs, release quickly. Repeat every 2 seconds. New method of artificial respiration	employed by fire department useful here.
Electric shock	Artificial respiration. Treat for shock.	Call veterinarian immediately.
Heat stroke	Quickly immerse the dog in cold water until relief is given. Give cold water enema. Or lay dog flat and pour cold water over him, turn electric fan on him, and continue pouring cold water as it evaporates.	Cold towel pressed against abdomen aids in reducing temp. quickly if quantity of water not available.
Porcupine quills	Tie dog up, hold him between knees, and pull all quills out with pliers. Don't forget tongue and inside of mouth.	See veterinarian to remove quills too deeply imbedded.
Shock	Cover dog with blanket. Administer stimulant (coffee with sugar). Allow him to rest, and soothe with voice and hand.	Alcoholic beverages are NOT stimulants.
Snake bite	Cut deep X over fang marks. Drop potassium-permanganate into cut. Apply tourniquet above bite if on foot or leg.	Apply first aid only if a veterinarian or a doctor can't be reached.

Remember that in most instances these are emergency measures, not specific treatments, and are designed to help you in aiding your pup until you can reach your veterinarian.

POISON	HOUSEHOLD ANTIDOTE
ACIDS	Bicarbonate of soda
ALKALIES	Vinegar or lemon juice
(cleansing agents)	
ARSENIC	Epsom salts
HYDROCYANIC ACID	Dextrose or corn sirup
(wild cherry; laurel leaves)	
LEAD	Epsom salts
(paint pigments)	
PHOSPHORUS	Peroxide of hydrogen
(rat poison)	
MERCURY	Eggs and milk
THEOBROMINE	Phenobarbital
(cooking chocolate)	
THALLIUM	Table salt in water
(bug poisons)	
FOOD POISONING	Peroxide of hydrogen, followed by
(garbage, etc.)	enema
STRYCHNINE	Sedatives. Phenobarbital, Nembutal.
DDT	Peroxide and enema

The important thing to remember when your dog is poisoned is that prompt action is imperative. Administer an emetic immediately. Mix hydrogen peroxide and water in equal parts. Force this mixture down your dog. In a few minutes he will regurgitate his stomach contents. Once this has been accomplished, call your veterinarian. If you know the source of the poison and the container which it came from is handy, you will find the antidote on the label. Your veterinarian will prescribe specific drugs and advise on their use.

The symptoms of poisoning include trembling, panting, intestinal pain, vomiting, slimy secretion from mouth, convulsions, coma. All these symptoms are also prevalent in other illnesses, but if they appear and investigation leads you to believe that they are the result of poisoning, act with dispatch as described above.

GLOSSARY

Action: the manner of a dog's movement.

AKC: American Kennel Club.

Alter: to remove the testes of the male or the ovaries of the female; to castrate or spay.

American Kennel Club: founded in 1884, the largest and most influential dog organization in the United States. It is actually an association of about 300 smaller clubs, either national one-breed clubs or regional multi-breed clubs. Parent clubs within the AKC establish breed standards which the AKC then maintains. The AKC serves as a registering organization for the breeds it recognizes to insure the legitimacy of pedigrees.

Anorchid: male dogs in which no testes have descended into the scrotum. Anorchids are usually referred to as cryptorchids by dog fanciers. See cryptorchid; monorchid.

B. or b.: See bitch.

Backcrossing: to breed a crossbred dog back to one of its parents or to a dog of the same breed as the parent.

Bat ear: a broad erect ear, as in the French Bulldog.

Beard: thick, heavy whiskers.

Belton: ticking in an English Setter.

Bench show: a conformation show; a show where dogs are kept on stall-like benches. See unbenched.

Bitch: the female dog; often abbreviated B. or b.

Bite: the manner in which the upper and lower teeth meet when the jaws are closed. See level bite; overshot; scissors bite; undershot.

Bloodlines: the lineage, or line of descent, of a family of dogs or of an individual dog.

Bloom: the shiny, glossy appearance of a coat.

Brace: a pair of dogs.

Broken color: a solid color interrupted by the addition of white.

Brood bitch: a bitch used for breeding.

Butterfly nose: a dark-colored nose with flesh-colored spots.

Button ear: an erect ear whose upper portion folds down in front of the ear opening, as typified by the Fox Terrier. See semiprick ear.

Castration: removal of the gonads; can pertain to either sex, but more commonly applied to altering of the male. See altering.

Catalog: a publication listing all the dogs entered in a particular dog show, pertinent information about these dogs, and the show schedule. See premium list.

Cat foot: a paw having a short, round, and compact appearance.

C.D.: companion dog.

C.D.X.: companion dog excellent.

Ch.: abbreviation for champion.

Champion: show: a dog awarded 15 show points, which include at least two major wins under different judges. Field: a gun dog earning a specific number of points and wins at field trials, the specific number varying between the pointing breeds, spaniels, retrievers, and hounds.

China eye: a wall eye with a clear blue iris.

Chromosomes: the twisted ladder-like elements in the nucleus of a body cell carrying the hereditary characters. See gene.

Cobby: a short compact body.

Colostrum: the "first" milk produced by the female for a short time after the birth of the young. It differs from the later milk in having a higher concentration of proteins, vitamins, minerals, and protective antibodies, and being lower in fats and sugars.

Companion dog: an obedience title awarded for passing three qualifying trials in novice class competition.

Companion dog excellent: an obedience title awarded for passing three qualifying trials in open class competition. Dogs must have previously earned C.D.

Conformation: the structure of the dog.

Coupling: the length of body between the forelegs and hindlegs.

Cropping: cutting and trimming the flesh of a drop-type ear to induce the remaining portion to stand erect.

Crossbreed: the offspring of two purebred dogs of different breeds.

Crossbreeding: the crossing of two purebred dogs of different breeds.

Croup: the rump; the area just in front of the tail.

Cryptorchid: a male dog in which only one or no testis has descended into the scrotum. Dog fanciers, however, commonly apply this term only to those males with *no* descended testes. See anorchid; monorchid.

D. or d.: See dog.

Dam: the female parent.

Dappled: irregular light and dark markings.

Dewclaws: the "thumb" and "big toe" of dogs, located a short distance above the paw. Anatomically, dogs walk on their fingertips and toes; the dewclaws are the "thumb" and "big toe" carried a short distance above the ground. See hock; pastern.

Docking: cutting a dog's tail to a shorter length.

Dog: (1) the domestic dog; a member of the species *Canis famili-*

aris; (2) certain wild canids, as the Cape hunting dog; (3) the male of the domestic dog, often abbreviated D. or d.

Double coat: a coat consisting of a soft thick undercoat and a coarse outercoat.

Down in pastern: when the angle formed between the pastern, the part of the leg just above the paw, and the ground is smaller than desired. See pastern.

Drop ear: an ear that hangs down and close to the head, as in most hounds and spaniels.

Dudley nose: a flesh-colored nose.

Elbow: the foreleg joint close to and just below the body.

Elbows out: See out at elbows.

Estrum: See estrus.

Estrus: the period in the female reproductive cycle when sexual excitability and ovulation occur; estrum.

Even bite: See level bite.

Fawn: a light yellow-tan.

Feathers: the fringe of long hair on the ears, legs, lower body, or tail of certain breeds.

Feet east and west: when the paws are naturally positioned turned out from the body.

Felted coat: a coat densely matted with wads of hair.

Femur: the thigh bone; the bone of the upper thigh in dogs.

Fiddle front: out at elbows, pastern joints turned in, feet east and west.

Flag: a tail carrying long hair, as in setters.

Flank: the loin and upper thigh.

Flat-sided: rib cage not adequately rounded.

Flews: the overhang of the upper lips, particularly at the corners of the mouth, as in Bloodhounds.

Forearm: the part of the foreleg between the elbow and pastern.

Foundation stock: the original dogs used by a kennel or breeder in establishing a new line or breed.

Full eye: a round, slightly bulbous eye.

Furnishings: the thick fringes of hair of a dog's coat, as whiskers, ear fringes, etc.

Gay tail: a tail carried well above the top of the back.

Gene: a segment of a chromosome carrying a specific hereditary characteristic. See chromosome.

Germ cells: sperm or egg cells, or the cells from which they develop.

Germ Plasm: (1) the cells from which the sperm and egg cells develop; (2) the sperm and egg cells; (3) genes. Definition (1) is preferred.

Get: offspring.

Gonads: the sex glands: testes and ovaries.

Goose rump: a rump with too much slope.

Ground color: the main background color of a multi-colored dog.

Hare foot: a long narrow paw.

Harelip: a congenital deformity in which the upper lip is split to the nose.

Haw: the nictitating membrane, a thin reddish membrane found beneath the lower eyelid.

Heat: the bitch's season; the estrus, or estrum, portion of the estrous cycle. Biologists generally use this term to refer only to the short acceptance phase during the female's cycle when she will actually accept males. See estrus.

Height: the measurement of a dog from his withers to the ground.

Hock: the joint between the lower thigh and pastern. Anatomically, dogs walk on their fingertips and toes; the hock is merely the raised heel of the hind foot. See dewclaws; pastern.

Hock well let down: sloping rear pastern, resulting in hock being closer to the ground than desired. See hock; pastern.

Humerus: the bone of the upper arm.

Inbreeding: the breeding of closely related dogs, as members of the same immediate family.

Iris: a circular muscle, containing pigments that give the eye its color, that regulates the size of the light opening, or pupil, of the eye.

Knee: the dog's pastern joint. The dog's "elbow" corresponds to the "knee" of human beings. See pastern.

Knuckled over: the bending forward of the pastern joint (wrist) of the foreleg.

Level bite: when the upper and lower front teeth meet edge to edge.

Line breeding: the breeding of related dogs, but not members of the same immediate family.

Listing fee: the nominal fee charged dog owners for entering a non-registered dog in a dog show.

Loin: the side of the body between the last rib and the hind legs.

Lower thigh: the hind leg from the stifle to the hock; the tibia.

Major win: a show win of 3 to 5 points; 5 is the maximum number of points that can be awarded to a dog at a single AKC show.

Mask: dark shadings on the muzzle.

Merle: blue and gray marbled with black.

Mixed breed: generally, a dog that is a mixture of more than two breeds.

Molera: a corruption of the Spanish word *mollera;* a space at the juncture of certain skull bones which bone has failed to fill, instead the opening is covered by a tough membrane. Once quite common in Chihuahuas.

Mongrel: See mixed breed.

Monorchid: a male dog in which only one testis has descended into the scrotum. See anorchid; cryptorchid.

Muzzle: the part of the head in front of the eyes: the foreface.

Non-slip retriever: a dog that retrieves downed game on command; it does not hunt or flush game on its own.

Occiput: the upper peak of the skull between the ears.

Out at elbows: elbows turned out away from the body.

Outbreeding: the breeding of two unrelated dogs. See backcrossing; crossbreeding; inbreeding; outcrossing.

Outcrossing: the crossing of two unrelated dogs of the same breed.

Ovary: the female gonad; produces female hormone and egg cells.

Overshot: the upper jaw protruding beyond the lower jaw and the upper front teeth passing in front of the lower front teeth when the jaws are closed.

Ovulation: the discharge of egg cells from the ovary.

Pad: the thick cushiony sole of a dog's foot.

Paper foot: a paw with a thin flat pad.

Parent club: the first specialty club of a given breed admitted to the AKC.

Parti-color: a coat of two or more colors, each occurring as clearly defined markings.

Pastern: (1) the "knee" joint of dogs. The pastern joint corresponds to the "wrist" of human beings. Anatomically, dogs walk on their fingertips and toes, resulting in the pastern joint, or "wrist," being carried at a point above the ground. (2) The section of the foreleg between the pastern joint and the paw, and the section of the hindleg between the hock and the paw. See dewclaws; hock.

Pied: two or more colors occurring over large areas.

Pig jaw: See overshot.

Pincer bite: See level bite.

Plucking: removing dead or excess hair from a dog's coat.

Plume: a longhaired tail carried over the back.

Points: distinct but matching colors on the face, ears, legs, and tail.

Premium list: the listing of the prizes awarded and the judges officiating at a given show. See catalog.

Prick ear: a stiff erect ear, usually pointed at the tip, as in German Shepherds.

Racy: tall, lean, and long-legged.

Ram's nose: a moderate roman nose.

Ringtail: a tail that curls up and around to form an almost complete circle.

Roach back: a back whose upper surface forms an upward-curving arch from withers to tail.

Roman nose: a muzzle whose upper surface forms an upward-curving arch from stop to nostrils.

Rose ear: an ear whose upper portion folds back or away from the ear opening, exposing the insides of the ear, as in English Bulldog.

Second thigh: See lower thigh.

Scapula: the shoulder blade.

Scissors bite: where the back of the upper teeth just touch the front of the lower teeth when the jaws are closed.

Season: See estrus; heat.

Screw tail: a short twisted tail.

Scrotum: the sac containing the testes.

Self color: a coat of one solid color, with or without lighter shades of the same color.

Semiprick ear: an erect ear whose tip points forward and down, as in the collie. See button ear.

Shoulders: See withers.

Sickle tail: a long tail carried up and out in a semicircle.

Sire: the male parent.

Snipey: a pointed, narrow muzzle.

Spay: to remove the ovaries (and, generally, the uterus as well) of the female; to castrate the female.

Splay foot: a thin flat paw with spread out toes.

Spring of ribs: the amount of roundness of the rib cage.

Squirrel tail: a short tail carried up and forward.

Stern: the tail, mostly used in reference to hounds and other gun dogs.

Stifle: the joint above the hock on the hind leg, located between the upper thigh (femur) and the lower thigh (tibia).

Stop: the slope, or dip, where the forehead meets the muzzle.

Straight hocked: too little angle at the hocks; hind leg showing little or no bend at the hock joint when viewed from the side.

Stud: a male dog used for breeding.

Sway-backed: a dipping curvature of the back from withers to tail.

Team: a group of four closely matched dogs of the same breed entered as a group in a dog show. A team very rarely may consist of only three dogs.

Testis: the male gonad; produces male hormone and sperm.

Throaty: too much loose skin under the throat.

Tibia: a bone of the lower leg.

Ticking: a coat of white flecked with tiny markings of a darker color.

Topknot: a pronounced growth, or tuft, of hair on top of the head.

Trimming: clipping a dog's coat to a desired outline.

Tuck-up: the change from a deep rib cage to a shallow loin, as in the Greyhound.

Tulip ear: an erect ear whose sides are curled slightly forward.

U.D.: utility dog.

Unbenched show: A conformation show where the dogs need be on the grounds only when being judged.

Undershot: the lower jaw protruding beyond the upper jaw and the lower front teeth passing well in front of the upper front teeth when the jaws are closed.

Upper thigh the part of the hind leg from the hip joints to the stifle; the thigh; the femur. See lower thigh.

Utility dog: an obedience title awarded for passing three qualifying trials in the utility class. Dog must have previously earned C.D.X.

Wall eye: an eye with a solid blue iris or a blue iris streaked with black or brown. See china eye.

Weak in pastern: See down in pastern.

Well sprung: a well-rounded rib cage.

Wheelback: See roach back.

Whiskers: a downward growth of wiry hair from the muzzle.

Withers: the point on the back between the shoulder blades, located at the base of the neck. This is the point used in measuring a dog's height from the ground. Dog fanciers often speak of this as "shoulder height," but technically, as the shoulders are actually located on the side of the body at a point *below* the withers, this term is not correct and should not be used.

INDEX

254

255